# Spirituality and Pedagogy

# Spirituality and Pedagogy
Being and Learning in Sacred Spaces

*Marilyn Llewellyn*

Learning Moments Press
*Pittsburgh, PA*

Learning Moments Press
Pittsburgh, PA 15235

www.learningmomentspress.com

Copyright © 2017 by Marilyn Llewellyn
All rights reserved

Daniel Casebeer, Managing Editor

ISBN-13: 978-0-9976488-0-5

BISAC Subject: Education/Curriculum  EDU/008000
BISAC Audience 06 (Professional & Scholarly)

*I dedicate this book with love to my mother,
Adeline Loschiavo Llewellyn, my first and greatest teacher.*

# Contents

Foreword — i

Preface — 1

*Chapter 1*
Contemplation on Pedagogy — 9

*Chapter 2*
Contemplation on Spirituality — 19

*Chapter 3*
Contemplation on Faith in Classroom Relationships — 27

*Chapter 4*
Contemplation on a Praxis of Compassion — 53

*Chapter 5*
Contemplation on Revelation—Curriculum in Process — 71

*Chapter 6*
Contemplation on Being and Learning Together — 91

References — 105

*Maria Piantanida and Noreen B. Garman*

# Foreword

In *The Courage to Teach* noted educator Parker Palmer (1998) wrote, "…to teach is to create a space in which the community of truth is practiced" (p. 90). Written in what nostalgically seem the halcyon days of 1998, this view of teaching was difficult enough to enact then. Now, as the very foundations of civil discourse seem fractured almost beyond repair, what does it take to create such spaces? What constitutes truth in a society that seems increasingly divided along the fault-lines of race, religion, gender, and income? What constitutes "community" at a time when ideological factions hunker down and revile those in opposing camps? These are challenges facing our society at large, but they also play out in the smaller arena of classrooms. In public schools and college campuses, students have protested "hostile learning environments" created when teachers present ideas that challenge deeply ingrained assumptions. Even before the hate-full rhetoric of the 2016 presidential campaign, we encountered students who felt not only free, but entitled, to express prejudices against racial, religious, and gendered minorities. How, among the cross currents of hurt and grievance, can teachers create safe classroom spaces where students can engage thoughtfully and respectfully with those whose views differ from their own?

By drawing from her own experiences and those of others, Marilyn Llewellyn contemplates such questions in *Spirituality and Pedagogy: Being and Learning in Sacred Spaces*. Her aim is not to provide technical answers to intractable questions, but to offer a language for wrestling with them. In the pages that follow, Dr. Llewellyn exemplifies the courage required to enter into "an inner journey toward more truthful ways of seeing and being in the world" (p. 6). With gentleness, faith and compassion, she offers a counterpoint to the often strident and militant voices that demand change rather than nurture growth. By revealing her own failings, she opens spaces for students to be more vulnerable, a softening of stance that creates possibilities for new, often disquieting ideas to enter the conversation.

The research of distinguished MIT scholar Sherry Turkle (2015) adds another troubling dimension to the pedagogical dilemmas confronting teachers who value thoughtful classroom discourse. For over thirty years Turkle has been studying the effects of technology on communication, particularly the ubiquitous use of social media. For children who have grown up with smart phones, conversing through Twitter and Facebook have become the new norm. From middle school through graduate school, students express anxiety about engaging in face-to-face conversations where they have no opportunity to edit their comments, figure out what will place them in the most positive light, and elicit a reassuring deluge of "likes." As they work to avoid the unpredictable messiness of face-to-face conversation as well as the "boredom" associated with prolonged exchanges, these students fail to understand how ideas evolve through discourse. Perhaps most disturbing of all is the way in which conversing through social media has undermined the capacity for self-reflection and empathy. Given these considerations, the student responses to Llewellyn's contemplations may serve as helpful examples for conversation-avoidant students. They illustrate a capacity to resonate with the thoughts of others and exemplify the value of diverse, individual insights. And perhaps, at a most basic level, they offer the reassuring message, "It's not only possible, but exciting to add one's thoughts, feelings, and voice to complicated conversations."

## References

Palmer, P. J. (1998). *The courage to teach: Exploring the inner landscape of a teacher's life.* San Francisco: Jossey-Bass Publishers.

Turkle, S. (2015). *Reclaiming conversation: The power of talk in a digital age.* New York: Penguin Press.

# Preface

On the farthest end of my bookshelves sits a copy of Jonathan Kozol's (2011; 1995) book, *Amazing Grace*. Lined beside it are many other books that explore the growing injustices in American society and the world. Many of these books focus on the oppressive forces and destructive effects of racism, classism, and militarism in our world. At the opposite end of an adjacent bookshelf are books which include readings in spirituality as well as spirituality in relation to postmodern theologies, feminist theology, liberation theology, ecofeminism, and creation theology. Scattered in between are numerous education books, works on feminist theory, writings in philosophy, and favourite novels and poetry.

Taken individually these books and the various disciplines they represent provide a window into my interests and passions. They illustrate some of what shapes my world view. From another perspective, many of these books represent various discourse communities which offer critical ideas and a vital language with which to envision education differently, particularly in contrast as it presently exists in many schools in the United States.

Education today is marked by prescriptive and pre-packaged curriculum leaving teachers and students with less authority over their learning environments. In my work as a teacher educator, I constantly encounter books, in-service programs, DVDs, and Internet sites that are meant to influence and shape how teachers are to teach. These various texts often communicate a technical approach to education. Furthermore, as Cuban (2004) argues, language of accountability has become more and more pervasive since World War II and recently has taken on a renewed force. In this barren educational environment, the language of standards, assessments, achievement, teacher quality index, evidence-based practice, data-driven instruction, and effective teaching dominates the rhetoric of teacher education. This language leaves little room for teachers to imagine schools as places for nurturing possibility, creating community, and reverencing the mystery of each child.

Language profoundly shapes reality as well as what we come to know. As David Geoffrey Smith (1999) reminds us:

> Attempts to cast a mode of speaking which is neutral or value-free…miss an essential point, which is that to speak means to speak from a particular place and set of circumstances… An attention to language means also an attention to the life conditions of those dwelling in the language. (p. 113)

Rational technical language leaves little room for teachers to imagine how they can navigate existing educational worlds while bringing forth new worlds that are more fair and equitable places for children and teachers to dwell.

Dwayne Huebner (1995) contends that education should be concerned with and attend to the journey of the self. All that limits or interferes with this journey should be resisted—a refreshing and encouraging counterpoint to the madness of many current educational reform initiatives. Huebner is critical of the ways that educators describe what is happening in a person's life as "learning theory" or "developmental theory" (p. 18). These categories remove the journey of the self from its sacred realm and reduce it to a predictable and technical process. I can only imagine what he might say if he were alive today during this age when educational growth is measured by a test score, taken within a limited time, and on a narrow set of skills. This reductionist paradigm is far from Huebner's idea of education as a journey of the self. And it is far from mine.

**Purpose of the Book**

The purpose of this book is to contemplate the nature of pedagogical relationships through a language of spirituality. Spirituality is often narrowly equated with religion and religious belief. In its most authentic sense, however, the spiritual is the force of life within; it is who each of us is at our most fundamental and deepest center. Thus, a language of spirituality opens conversational spaces about teaching and learning that are proscribed by the technical language of accountability and achievement.

I do not presume that interjecting a language of spirituality into the discourses of teacher education will bring about sweeping reform in our society's structures of schooling. Such grandiosity is not the purpose of this book. Rather, my intent is to offer a language that allows teachers and teacher educators to express and explore the ineffable qualities of teaching and learning. Without such a language it is far too easy to lose sight of the very reason many of us are drawn to the teaching profession—a desire to make a difference in the lives of young people. One challenge of offering an alternative to a technological view of education is avoiding prescriptive language that inadvertently conveys a stance of advice-giving. To avoid this pitfall, I share narrative vignettes that I have crafted from my personal experience or from the experiences shared with me by others. Each vignette represents a "moment," a time of heightened significance that has stayed with me over the years. By sharing these moments, I invite readers to enter vicariously into events that have shaped so much of what I believe about classrooms as sacred space. It is my hope that these narrative glimpses into my life will evoke readers' memories of moments that have influenced who they are as teachers and learners.

During the course of my doctoral studies, I had an opportunity that is all too rare within the hectic pace of day-to-day teaching. I had time to contemplate what my recollected moments might tell me about myself as a teacher and a human being participating in the classroom lives of students. I offer these contemplations—not to reinvent or valorize the past—but to offer a spiritual language that might help readers gain new insights into their own pedagogical practice.

## A Note on the Concept of Contemplation

Contemplation is a way to enter deeply into a life event using imagination, thoughts and feelings. Contemplation is a way to hear, see, taste, smell, and touch embodied themes in order to distill the troubling issues, anomalies, and important aspects in pedagogical moments and life events that reveal potential. (Bevis, 1988) A central dimension of contemplation is awareness. Deep awareness can lead to an experience where the distance between oneself and that which one is gazing upon diminishes to such an extent that there is a unitive encounter. This encounter tends to differentiate contemplation somewhat from the experience of meditation which "is generally understood to involve discursive reasoning" (Downey, 1993, p. 209). In contemplation, an experience can occur where one lifts one's mind beyond itself to something or someone in such a way that it transcends itself and comes to taste a joy and deep heartfelt knowledge. In contemplation there is interrelatedness of mind, body, and spirit.

There is no single or prescriptive way to enter into contemplation. The process for me, however, does incorporate some common approaches. I begin by seeking to be open through a ritual or experience. Sometimes I sit quietly and try to come to a state of bodily calm in order to move into an inner stillness. Other times I put on some music and allow the rhythmic sounds to flow into my body. And, still at other times, physical movement enhances my capacity to enter fully into the contemplation.

When it seems appropriate, I choose some incident, pedagogical moment, or event. on which to focus. Through imagination and the use of my senses, I actively engage with it. I allow the text to speak to me, inviting me to "re-vision" in the sense that Adrienne Rich (1979) uses the word as "the act of looking back, of seeing with fresh eyes, of entering an old text from a new critical direction" (p. 35). Being open to the moment—seeing it with fresh eyes—allows the mystery of it to continually unfold. After spending a significant amount of time in this quiet contemplation, I usually write some of the thoughts, images and ideas that are revealed. By writing, I capture my thoughts while they are still vivid and create a text that I can revisit for further contemplation. The entire process requires openness to the notion that revelation occurs in multiple, mysterious, and natural ways. Consistent time

*Etymology of Contemplation*

The word contemplation derives from the Latin *templum*, translated as time. It is a diminutive of tempus and primarily used to express a separation, partition, or segment of time. In Greek the closest approximation to the word contemplation is *theoria* which comes from the verb *theorein* meaning to intently look at something for a purpose. For the Romans, *templum* designated the spatial and took the form of an actual space sectioned off for the augurs to read signs and omens gleaned from looking at the viscera of birds. The *templum* eventually came to be seen as a sacred place where holy persons prognosticated divine meanings they culled from signs or omens. While the temple was an actual place where sacred persons came to portend, predict, and give witness to divine promises, contemplation came to mean not a physical place but the act of beholding, gazing or looking attentively at the insides of something or someone (Downey, 1993).

spent in periods of contemplation and writing is vital if the revelation is to take shape.

This brief sketch of contemplation evokes images of quiet solitude. Indeed, for me this is an important aspect of grappling with complex ideas. But equally important for me are the many conversations I have with teaching colleagues and learners in my classrooms as I share my insights and writings. Through these dialogic opportunities new insights are gained and new questions generated. In considering a structure for this book, I wondered if there might be a way to give readers a flavor of both contemplative and dialogic experiences. This desire has given shape to the organizational structure of the book.

## Organization of the Book

Taken as a whole, this book is a contemplative text. In each chapter, I offer a contemplation on an aspect of *Spirituality and Pedagogy*.

In Chapter 1, a Contemplation on Pedagogy, I share the life context that engendered my initial understanding of the concept and my subsequent engagement with theoretic texts that deepened my early understandings. In Chapter 2, a Contemplation on Spirituality, I share my struggle to find a spiritual language that is not conflated with a language of narrow religiosity.

The next three chapters focus on qualities embodied within a pedagogy of spirituality. Chapter 3 introduces the quality of Faith in Classroom Relationships. Educational relationships rooted in faith defy expression in the technical language of behavioural objectives, standardized measurement, and lockstep progression toward prescriptive curriculum goals. Unlike pedagogical relationships based in an ideology of achievement, a relationship grounded in faith invites us to believe that the possibility for growth is always present in the other person and within oneself. It places the learner at the center of the learning process.

Chapter 4, Praxis of Compassion, explores issues of teaching authentically in an educational system (and society) that places a premium on assessment through standardized tests, order, competition, rewards, punishments and compliance. Giving witness to a praxis of compassion challenges teachers' very way of being in relationship with learners.

Chapter 5 begins with a recollection of a horrific event that revealed to me the depths of institutionalized injustice in our society. As I struggle to avoid the oppressive use of power in my own pedagogy, I explore the idea of Revelation—Curriculum in Process. Integral to this exploration is the issue of where and how knowledge is constructed. When teaching is no longer seen as simply disseminating material and repeating information, it requires imagination, energy, and vulnerability to create a context for generating discourse and creating knowledge.

Chapter 6 focuses on Being and Learning Together in Sacred Spaces. In this chapter I offer an explication of what I mean by sacred and how this connects to being and learning together. Drawing upon the wisdom of the ancients, I suggest that classrooms are rendered sacred when they become spaces where persons can use their power and engage in authentic learning. Within such spaces, wisdom and hope may be found. This wisdom encourages a view of curriculum and pedagogy as emerging as whole, first from our being; then from being with one another; and finally from being in the world. Centralized control and bureaucratic mandates directly contradict a spirituality of teaching in which the mystery and wonder of each person is of utmost importance. Creating community without diminishing the individual calls for responsiveness to the human condition within the here and now of the classroom. This is both the challenge and awe of the spirituality of pedagogy.

In Chapters 3 through 5, I offer narrative vignettes that portray a "moment." These moments are offered with no introduction, because I want readers to encounter them as they might if we were in conversation and I simply said, "Let me tell you about an experience that happened to me."

Following the vignettes, I offer my contemplations, as if I were responding to a conversational partner's question, "Well, what did you make of that?" Through these contemplations I probe the nuances of teacher-student relationships grounded in spirituality. In doing so, readers may gain new ways of interpreting moments from their own lives or be affirmed in their own values of teaching and learning.

For several years, I have shared the contemplations in Chapters 3, 4, and 5 with undergraduate students who were enrolled in my Curriculum Theory course. At times the students read one of the contemplations and wrote a reflection on the piece. At other times, reading was followed by classroom discussion, and then an invitation to write a piece to be shared in class. As part of their end-of-semester reflections, students would often choose to comment on one or more of the contemplations, which they often referred to as "articles." I have included a sampling of the students' responses to add a dialogic dimension to the book. Adding these glimpses of student thinking is risky, because they are disconnected from multifaceted conversations that took place over the course of a semester. This risk has been outweighed, however, by a desire to expand the body of ideas available for readers to contemplate.

**Audience for the Book**

As mentioned above, the purpose of this book is to contemplate the nature of pedagogical relationships through a language of spirituality. My hope is that other teachers and teacher educators will find these contemplations not simply interesting but evocative. Individuals might embark on a contemplative process of their own—setting aside time each day or week—to quietly revisit moments contained in this book or moments from their own lives. Teacher educators may choose to share the contemplations with their students as a catalyst for class discussion. However readers choose to engage with this text, I have written it with a spirit of faith and hope in the capacity of compassionate teachers to make a difference in the lives of students.

*Chapter 1*

# Contemplation on Pedagogy

As I contemplate my evolving understanding of pedagogy, it is important to acknowledge that my initial exposure to the concept was not through teacher education courses focused on instructional strategies and techniques. Rather, I first encountered the word pedagogy in a context where theory and action were integrated into my life. My first conscious recollection of the concept came when I read Paulo Freire's (1970) book, *Pedagogy of the Oppressed*, sometime in the early 1970s. At the time, I was living in a convent and working on my undergraduate degree in history and education. Persons who lived in the community surrounding the convent were predominantly African-Americans. During these years I took the Book Mobile to residents at the Kelly Street high-rise and spent hours listening to the rich stories that people shared with me about their lives. I also worked with various parish and neighborhood groups and participated in a number of committees.

There was a good deal of diversity within these groups, and we struggled to work in collegial and collaborative ways. The leadership was exercised by persons who were black—a new experience for someone who grew up white in a racially segregated society. Although some of my earlier life experiences had slowly shaped a critical consciousness in me, it was not until I lived in a racially and economically diverse social context that I began to confront my hidden assumptions and ignorance. Eventually, reading Carter G. Woodson's (1933/1993), *The Mis-education of the Negro*, exposed the depths of my own mis-education, including a limited exposure to history and literature that reflected the many voices and cultures in our world. Such experiences set in motion a lifelong process of re-education, and in this regard my introduction to critical pedagogy through the work of Paulo Freire was very influential. For Freire education is a political act interconnected with pedagogy.

Learning about *conscientization* and engaging in action that was shaped by reflection and then re-shaped by further action invited me into a pedagogical framework that was both challenging and liberating. The Portuguese term conscientização was popularized by Freire in *Pedagogy of the Oppressed*. Translated into English as "conscientization" and better known as "consciousness raising" and "critical consciousness," it is a socio-political educative method that invites learners into a critical reflection on the nature of their social, economic and historical reality through the cyclical process of reflection and action. For Freire, the goal of critical consciousness is for persons to act as knowing subjects in the creation of their future by recognizing and addressing the social, economic and political contradictions affecting them. Conscientization includes taking action against oppressive dimensions in one's life that are a result of that understanding. Freire's work helped me to understand ways to allow change to emerge from the group rather than imposing an already established structure on the group.

This was a valuable lesson in understanding *praxis* and influenced the way I would be in the classroom. Praxis is the conjunction of theory and practice—here practice and theory arise out of one another. It is the act of reflecting, engaging, applying and acting in an on-going cyclical manner in order to uncover real problems and their causes. It aims to change things in response to actual needs as opposed to reproducing the status quo. Within the realm of education, Freire envisioned intergenerational equity between teachers and students whereby both question, reflect, and learn in such a way as to participate in meaning-making together.

Cognitive science has been dominated by a model of cognition that correlated the workings of the human mind with the workings of a computer. Here information processing is equated with knowing and "cognition is a representation of an independently existing world" (Capra, p. 270). One way that this framework of cognition has influenced education and schooling is through what Paulo Freire (1970) criticized as the "banking method." Knowledge is seen as a body of facts and information that the teacher deposits into the empty account or mind of the learner. The knowledge is held in the learner's mind until it is needed. At this point it is simply withdrawn and used much in the same way that money is deposited and withdrawn for use in a capitalist system. In this model of cognition, knowledge is viewed as part of an objective and independently existing world.

The Santiago theory has posed a challenge to these previously held theories of cognition. In the Santiago theory

> ...cognition is not a representation of an independent, pregiven world, but rather a bringing forth of a world. What is brought forth by a particular organism in the process of living is not *the* world but *a* world, one that is always dependent upon the organism's structure. Since individual organisms within a species have more or less the same structure, they bring forth similar worlds. We humans, moreover, share an abstract world of language and thought through which we bring forth our world together. (Capra, p. 270)

Other readings helped me to explore and expand my understanding of critical pedagogy. Contributing to my re-education were works on liberation theology that were coming out of Latin America as well as material on black theology being written by persons such as James Cone (1969) and Albert Cleage (1968). Some documents within the framework of Catholic Social Teaching were also very influential in shaping my thinking during the 1970's and beyond.

Although I had encountered feminist literature at this time, it was later, during my doctoral work that I became aware of the growing body of literature written by women in the areas of feminist and womanist liberation theology, and black feminist thought related to spirituality and pedagogy.[1] It was at this time that I also became acquainted with authors writing more specifically about feminist pedagogy as a way of being with students in classrooms and as a field of study. Jennifer Gore's (1993) book, *The Struggle for Pedagogies,* offered a helpful exploration of the roots of feminist pedagogy.

> Women's Studies courses and departments on university campuses emerged out of the women's liberation movement, a social and political movement that has a long history of struggle. Writers of feminist pedagogy who are located in these departments, tend to emphasize the instructional processes of teaching, focusing on pedagogy in terms of *how* to teach and *what* to teach…thus the pedagogy argued for centers on discussions of classroom processes and principles. (p.20)

Kathleen Weiler (1991) also points to the ways in which feminist pedagogy resisted entrenched beliefs about what should be taught and processes for teaching:

> These developments within universities—the institutionalization of women's studies as programs and departments and the challenge to existing canons and disciplines by the new scholarship on women and by feminist theory—are reflected in the classroom teaching methods that have come to be loosely termed feminist pedagogy. (p. 455)

---

[1] I have been drawn particularly to works by Penny Lernoux (1989), Delores Williams (1993), Diana Hayes (Hayes, 1995), Elizabeth Schüssler Fiorenza (1996), Katie Cannon (1988), Youtha Hardman-Cromwell (1995), Marcia Riggs (1994), Rosemary Radford Ruether (Radford Ruether, 1992, 1996), Emilie Townes (1993; 1995), Gloria Joseph (1995), Barbara Omolade (1993), bell hooks (1984), Anna Julia Cooper (1988) and others.

Gore contends that within Education Departments, feminism was assigned a central place while issues of pedagogical practice that would focus on bringing feminism into the educational process were left pretty much unaddressed, because Education Departments bring a

> ...long history of educational thought and practice to questions of feminist pedagogy, a history that has been dominated by scientism, professionalism, technical rationality, patriarchy. Feminist pedagogy emerged in Education from a growing discontent with the patriarchy of schooling and with mainstream and radical masculinist educational discourses, the analyses of which were clearly connected to and resonant with the feminist movement(s). This strand of feminist pedagogy largely rejects the more technical, instructional meaning of pedagogy: pedagogy as a method of teaching within a context of awareness of women's oppression and a commitment to ending it. Pedagogy is instead approached more broadly, emphasizing how gendered knowledge and experience are produced. (pp. 25-26)

In her review of the literature, Gore concludes that there are many feminist pedagogies not just one. Similarly, Julie Brown (1992) observes, "Feminist pedagogy is still defining itself, largely through a process of questioning long standing beliefs and practices in education" (p. 52) and "no single definition of feminist pedagogy exists" (p. 60). While there is no one definition of feminist pedagogy, some frameworks related to dimensions of feminist pedagogy have been offered. For Jennifer Gore pedagogy includes "both instruction and social vision" (p. 4) and

> ...the discourse of feminist pedagogy attends to aspects of content and aspects of classroom processes, with the emphasis on processes...In terms of content, three main approaches...

are evident: (1) presenting "new" texts, previously marginalized or overlooked within disciplinary knowledge; (2) engaging in "new readings" of old texts...; (3) drawing on the personal experiences of teacher and students as the basis of knowledge production. (pp. 78-79)

Carolyn Shrewsbury (1993) contends that "at its simplest level, feminist pedagogy is concerned with gender justice and overcoming oppression" (p. 9). Shrewsbury claims that feminist pedagogy can transform education for both men and women through three central concepts of community, leadership, and empowerment. Feminist pedagogy is about creating classrooms where communities of learners have opportunities to exercise personal autonomy and collegiality that is responsive to all involved.

Within the realm of feminist pedagogy, classroom practices challenge traditional hierarchical arrangements and competitive structures by emphasizing cooperation, interaction and collaboration. Evaluation methods also depart from traditional letter or numerical grading, which are often determined by measuring one learner against another. Non-didactic approaches, including discussion, role play, journal writing and storytelling are core to evaluation in feminist pedagogy. These practices are often aimed at forming connections—among class participants, between people with different experiences and different "subjectivities," between the private realm of mothering and the public, between the private and public worlds of each woman (Grumet, 1988). For Weiler (1991), "Looking to experience as the source of knowledge and the focus of feminist learning is perhaps the most fundamental tenet of feminist pedagogy" (p. 465).

Through on-going efforts to counteract the mis-education of my youth, I have come to see critical consciousness—not strategy, method or technique—as the heart and soul of my pedagogy. In a 1919 lecture, Rudolf Steiner (1995), founder of the Waldorf School, spoke of pedagogy in the following way:

For the true teacher, pedagogy must be something living, something new at each moment. We could even say that the best pedagogy is one that the teacher continually forgets and that is continually reignited each time the teacher is in the presence of the children and sees in them the living powers of developing human nature. (p. 31)

Similarly, Max van Manen (1991) offers thoughts on the human dimensions of good pedagogy:

A sense of vocation, love of and caring for children, a deep sense of responsibility, moral intuitiveness, self-critical openness, thoughtful maturity, tactful sensitivity toward the child's subjectivity, an interpretive intelligence, a pedagogical understanding of the child's needs, improvisational resoluteness in dealing with young people, a passion for knowing and learning the mysteries of the world, the moral fibre to stand up for something, a certain understanding of the world, active hope in the face of prevailing crises, and, not the least, humor and vitality. (p. 8)

Steiner's and van Manen's conceptions of pedagogy stand in contrast to much of the literature within the field of education. Erica McWilliam's (1996) contends that within much education writing, teaching has been removed from pedagogy in favour of a design-delivery system. She writes:

Increasingly, educational arrangements which are founded on this bifurcation of teaching and learning threaten to erase the notion of 'teaching' altogether. At the very least, we are witnessing in the burgeoning academic work on 'open learning' a preference for substituting the term 'delivery' for teaching, and/or the substitution of 'instructional designer' for 'teacher.' Just as the 'teacher' is in decline as an object of educational inquiry, the term 'pedagogy' is making an appearance as a concept that endorses such an erasure, rather than troubling it.

"Teaching" has been displaced as part of the binary system of talking educational practice. This displacement has been made possible through the bifurcation of teaching into 'design and delivery.' In turn, both design and delivery are held to be the outcomes of particular organizational and management processes and strategies. What is flagged here is the need to construct a more efficient loop from academic manager to instructional designer to 'deliver' to learner, and (feed)back to academic manager.

This construction of pedagogy as a cycle of information in a one-way flow (design-deliver-evaluate-re-design), stands in contrast to the way the term "pedagogy" is employed elsewhere in the humanities and social sciences. 'One-way' pedagogy does not address knowledge production as distinct from information dissemination and consumption, necessarily relational and dynamic as a form of cultural exchange. In the new educational literature reference to the learner/student as a "client" of the educational institution certainly maintains the notion of 'pedagogy' as relational, but it is a relationship that is increasingly held to be directly synonymous with that of 'producer and/or consumer' in commerce and industry. (pp. 2-3)

When viewed in this way, pedagogy contributes to a growing functionalism in our schools which, from a critical consciousness standpoint, needs to be challenged.

Ultimately, pedagogy implies the relational process that happens in the classroom. It is how we look upon one another and how we communicate that to each other. Pedagogy involves determining what is considered knowledge, how knowledge is constructed, and what is valued as a way of knowing. Pedagogy is a way of knowing and a way of being. They are intimately connected to and inseparable from each another. Within this view of pedagogy, the functional language—of design and delivery, of order and management, of power and control—is not adequate. Such language excludes the ineffable magic between teachers and learners who engage authentically in classroom spaces. In the next chapter, I contemplate the potential for a language of spirituality to express the inexpressible.

*Chapter 2*

# Contemplation on Spirituality

Much in teaching is inexpressible. Yet within the realm of the spiritual, I have found a vital, even mythic, language that helps to express a way of being in the world. This language embodies a way of knowing that can shape transformative possibilities in being together as teachers and learners in classroom spaces.

As with any powerful concept, spirituality holds many different meanings depending on one's beliefs and values. All too often, however, spirituality is narrowly equated only with religion and religious belief. I avoid (and at times am even repulsed by) fundamentalist religious language. I am suspicious of and reject a Euro-centric male theology and spirituality with doctrines and ideologies that are deeply embedded in exclusionary and oppressive language. I also find the language used by some religious groups to be deterministic, judgmental, and essentialist. At times, there seems to be a lack of connection between religion and concern for persons in our world who are suffering from injustices. Therefore, I resist using any language that resembles this narrow form of religiosity. Nor do I use a traditionally spiritual language in speaking. Nonetheless, I experience a deep connection to the spiritual; it gives meaning to my life and is, in essence, an expression of who I am. In its most authentic sense, the spiritual is the force of life within; it is who each of us is at our most fundamental and deepest center.

Thus, spiritual language can transcend the narrow and utilitarian goal of schooling so often associated with preparing young people for the workforce. As educator Noreen Garman (1994) states:

> We are being challenged to pay attention to how language influences the thought and conduct of those we work with, and more important, what our language tells us about our own dispositions and motives. (p.1)

Exploring the spirituality of teaching and learning is a way to envision pedagogy differently from education rooted in medical, business, or technological paradigms. Frances Schoonmaker (2009) refers to spirituality as "a way of being that includes the capacity of humans to see beyond ourselves, to become more than we are, to see mystery and wonder in the world around them, and to experience private and collective moments of awe, wonder, and transcendence" (p. 2714). By drawing on the spiritual, we can begin to imagine schools as places where education is seen as a journey into a deeper and fuller life; a space in which to express one's being. When we understand spirituality in the classroom as a connection between being and knowing, then the act of learning is more than measurable objectives.

Joel Kovel (1991) espouses a belief in "spirituality's central place in human existence" (p. 8) and the idea "that there is a quality, best called spiritual, which characterizes human beings and cannot be explained away psychologically; that is, there is a spiritual component to human nature" (p. 13). When spirit is seen as the force that gives life to physical organisms, it offers compelling images of connection, vitality and possibility. Kovel's work illustrates that spirit and spirituality encompasses much more than religion. He contends that

> ...what we call "spirit" occurs in the motion of the dialectic, as splitting is overcome, and in relation to the liberation of nature. Spirit is not opposed to matter, or the flesh; rather it is revealed, indeed created, in the freeing of matter and flesh; that is, in the overcoming of splitting. And spirit is not a by-product, or an indicator, of this overcoming; it is the lived process itself. Thus liberation is a spiritual project, and spirituality is emancipatory. (p. 3)

Within this view of spirit, spirituality is embedded in "every sphere of existence" (p. 4). This points to a view of cognition and the mind that is markedly different from that espoused by behavioural psychology, neurophysiology, and other scientific disciplines that seek to understand the mind only as an artefact of bio-chemical processes and anatomical structures. Indeed, as Fritjof Capra (1996) points out, identifying the mind with "the process of life is a radically new idea in science, but it is also one of the deepest and most archaic intuitions in humanity. In ancient times the rational human mind was seen as merely one aspect of the immaterial soul, or spirit" (p. 264). In elaborating on this idea, Capra draws on the work of Humberto Maturana and Francisco Varela,[1] two philosophers associated with the Santiago theory of cognition. He explains:

In the emerging theory of living systems, mind is not a thing, but a process. It is cognition, the process of knowing, and is identified with the process of life itself. (p. 264)

Capra goes on to point out that the basic distinction that surfaced was between body/soul or body/spirit, not between mind and body. Soul and spirit "originally unified in themselves two concepts—that of force of life and that of activity of consciousness" (p. 264).

Capra explains how the metaphor "breath of life" best expresses the unified concepts of "force of life" and "activity of consciousness" found within the etymological meanings of soul and spirit. In various languages of ancient times, the etymological roots of both soul and spirit mean breath. Capra claims that the "common ancient intuition behind all these words is that of soul or spirit as the breath of life" and that this can be seen as similar to the Santiago theory in that the "concept of cognition...goes far beyond the rational mind, as it includes the whole process of life. Describing it as the breath of life is a perfect metaphor" (p. 256). Viewed in this way the

---

1  For further information on the Santiago Theory of Cognition see Humberto R. Maturana and Francisco J. Varela, (1980) *Autopoiesis and Cognition: The Realization of the Living*.

process of knowing is the process of life and living itself. To the extent that teachers are responsible for supporting processes of knowing, they are ethically obligated to respect each student as a living being on a journey of and toward the self. It is not enough to say, "I am here only to convey information about math or science or reading or English or history or any other subject." Within classroom spaces, the processes of knowing and life become intertwined. The very act of teachers' and students' being together infuses pedagogy with a spiritual dimension.

> *Etymological Connection between Spirit & Breath*
>
> The Greek word for spirit and soul is *pneuma* meaning breath or wind. The Latin word for soul is *anima*, meaning breath, and the Latin word for spirit is *spiritus*, again meaning breath. Also, the Hebrew word for spirit is *ruah* and the Sanskrit word for soul is *atman*, both meaning breath (Oxford English Dictionary).

This is a strange perspective in a modern, secular society where the social order functions independently from the spiritual realm. From the dawn of the modern era, a view that reason and the secular social order could address and solve societal problems progressively took shape. Gradually, however, an exclusively secular foundation for society—marked by dualisms, positivism, scientism, and instrumental rationality—is being challenged. Edith Wyschogrod (1990) suggests that the postmodern era came into being with a "death event." The reality of Auschwitz became the metaphor for an all pervasive devaluing of life on a global scale, and with the use of atomic weapons and the rapid technological development that followed, the modern era wanes and the postmodern era comes into being. This framework is not meant to suggest that an event begins or ends an historical era, but rather it suggests that events, as horrific and tragic as Auschwitz, are also metaphors that represent major shifts in worldview. Ann Astell (1996/Summer) contends that "Auschwitz teaches us the horrific lessons of 'either-or,' showing us how easily idols of modernity—individualism, equality, freedom, rationality, and progress—turn into their opposites: hateful division, massification, slavery, tyranny, brutality, and death" (p. 5).

Postmodern sensibility tends toward a view of spirituality as being integrally concerned with what is real in society. This concern extends to economic, political, and social issues, but with the view that spirituality offers a hope for social change when spiritual concerns are seen as interconnected with societal realities. The separation of church and state, sacred and profane, secular and spiritual are deeply embedded in modernist thinking. In contrast, a central dimension of postmodern spirituality is its emphasis on "relations as internal, essential, and constitutive. An individual does not first exist as a self-contained entity with various qualities on the basis of which he or she then has superficial interactions with other beings which do not affect his or her essence. The relations one has with one's body, one's larger natural environment, one's family, and one's culture are instead constitutive of one's very identity"(Griffin, 1988, p. 14). Postmodern spirituality draws meaning from the postmodern science of deep ecology and quantum physics which offers new understandings of the universe. Postmodern spirituality challenges the separation between the sacred and the secular, and it rejects modern materialism as well as modern dualism, a view of humans as separated from nature. An additional feature of postmodern spirituality is a stress on a postpatriarchal vision (Griffin, 1988).

Unfortunately, schools as social institutions were shaped within a modernist world view with its many perceived dualisms and dichotomies. In many instances, this extended the separation of secular and spiritual into education. Dwayne Huebner's (1975a, 1975b, 1975c, 1983, 1984; 1985, 1995; 1999a, 1999b) extensive work in the area of spirituality and education has pushed the boundaries by placing talk of the spiritual and spirituality as a focus of curriculum theorizing. Huebner (1985) points out

> Talk of the "spirit" and the "spiritual" in education need not…
> be God talk, even though the traditions wherein "spiritual" is
> used most frequently are religious traditions. Rather, the talk
> is about lived reality, about experience and the possibility
> of experiencing. Another sphere of being is not referred to.
> The "spiritual" is of this world, not of another world; of this
> life, not of another life. But the spiritual is not necessarily
> contained, nor even acknowledged, in the way that we
> presently know and live in this world. (p. 164)

In the 1985 yearbook publication, *Learning and Teaching the Ways of Knowing*, edited by Elliot Eisner (1985) and put out by the National Society for the Study of Education, Huebner joins with other educators to advance the dialogue around various ways of knowing. These include: aesthetic modes of knowing, scientific knowing, interpersonal modes of knowing, intuitive knowing, narrative and paradigmatic modes of thought, formal modes of knowing, practical modes of knowing, and spiritual ways of knowing. In saying this, educational concepts and constructs cannot ignore spirituality. Spirituality and education can be in dialogue with each other in order to shape new horizons.

Huebner's focus on spirituality as a mode of knowing within the context of education is related to spirituality as pedagogy. At its most fundamental level, spirituality as pedagogy is about ways of being together in the overall process of living and learning. In the context of schooling, the original concern begins with the mystery and wonder of the person. As the mystery unfolds there is a growing reverence for the person and the understanding that, since we can never completely know another person, the possibility of surprise and hope for newness is always present. Thus, this encompasses an utter concern for the person, creating community without diminishment of the individual, and responding to the human condition present in the here and now. These are core dimensions of spirituality as pedagogy.

In suggesting that there are essential aspects of spirituality as pedagogy, it also is important to acknowledge that the social and cultural context particular to each school is unique. Therefore, spirituality as pedagogy is a way of being where what is real in the here and now, particularly the context of the school and classroom, determines the kind of response and action that is needed. Centralized control and bureaucratic directions are in direct contradiction to spirituality as pedagogy. Universal mandates that are in conflict with what is real must be rejected in favour of creating educational directions together that are mutual and have the potential to be transforming for all. Spirituality as pedagogy requires transgression on behalf of justice. It calls forth from us the difficult work of challenging the power structures in the school and the classroom that keep young persons oppressed and in the margins. Finally, spirituality as pedagogy is a way of being that embodies love and compassion.

Condensed in this way, spirituality as pedagogy seems daunting, and indeed it can be. But often spirituality as pedagogy is enacted in small ways—in moments when we have a choice about how to respond; how to be with another. As I reflect on my own life—as teacher and student—I see the ways in which such moments have shaped who I am and want to be as a teacher. In the following chapters, I share a number of moments that have had a profound influence on me. In drawing upon the events of my life's journey, I want to emphasize that what I say in this book is not the result of a linear progression of experiences culminating in insight about the current state of education.

Rather, the whole book serves as a kairotic contemplation. This concept itself is illustrative of the spiritual language I bring to my understanding of education. Drawn from spiritual traditions, kairos is an expression of time as a period of significance, a fulfilled moment or event that makes a difference in one's life. Unlike chronological time which is seen as sequential and unbroken, kairos is an expression of decisive time, the fullness of time, or the coming into being of a new state. Laurel Richardson (1990) refers to the work of philosopher

Edmund Husserl in expressing an understanding of kairos in this manner:

> Unlike the clock and calendars that measure out life in moments, days and years, people do not experience time as a succession of instants or a linear linking of points in space but as extended awareness of the past and the future within the present. (p. 208)

I use the concept of kairos as an organizing principle in this book to reconstruct the life events that form the extended awareness of the past and the future within the present leading to new ways of being. Within the ordinariness of day-to-day living, many events have shaped and continue to shape my spirituality and pedagogy. As Huebner (1975b) reminds me:

> Human life is not futural; nor is it past, but rather, a present made up of a past and future brought into the moment...Human life is never fixed but is always emergent as the past and future become horizons of present. (p. 244)

As a kairotic contemplation, this book allows me to express my life events, not as chronological, singular, fixed or isolated, but rather as emergent, interrelated, evolving out of and intertwining with one another. Many aspects related to life can often remain concealed through deliberate design, possible necessity, or simple lack of awareness. In writing this book, it is my hope to open a window into what is not so readily visible about how vital a spirituality of teaching and learning might be today.

*Chapter 3*

# Contemplation on Faith in Classroom Relationships

### A Moment: My First Parent-Teacher Conference

I walked to school that crisp autumn morning filled with a mixture of excitement, anxiety and fear. It was my first year of teaching, and today was my initiation into parent/teacher conferences. I was certain the parents would make many criticisms of me. As I nervously waited for my first parent to arrive, I thought of how my life had turned out differently from what I had expected.

I had switched from an elementary education major and sociology minor during my junior year of college to a history major and secondary education minor. I did my student teaching in the early 1970's in an urban Catholic high school for girls. After my first day of student teaching, the teacher with whom I worked said that she would like me to be responsible for three of her social studies classes; she gave me the textbooks for the freshman and sophomore classes and told me to prepare lessons for the next day. I went home and spent the evening figuring out how I would present the material for these history classes. Following the homeroom period the next morning, I stepped up to the front of the room and began the lesson. After the first 10 minutes, the teacher went out of the room and left me to conduct the class by myself, as she would every day for the entire semester. I struggled to make the material interesting. I tried to create a fun and relaxed atmosphere while retaining some semblance of order and control. I learned so much about teaching during those five months, and I was convinced that I should continue to teach high school students.

However, I ended up teaching sixth grade at the urban elementary school where I now sat waiting for parents to arrive. Sitting there, I remembered how unprepared I had been for elementary teaching—but under the guidance of some excellent teachers in the school, I had come a long way.

When I had prepared my classes in August, I was not aware that it was the norm to place students into ability-based reading groups, and so every day we did some activity in language arts that defied the need for any arbitrarily assigned groupings based on skill assessments. We read recipes (and then made fudge), mapped trips across the United States on the floor, played grammar games, wrote creative writing exercises, group poetry, limericks and drama—activities that allowed great diversity in the student groupings.

I had ignored the conventional wisdom "don't smile until Christmas," taking the chance that if I allowed the students to laugh and enjoy themselves, perhaps I would not spend the rest of the year trying to regain control. It was a struggle. I made plenty of mistakes. However, I continually learned from the students. One teacher also helped me a great deal with the content of my classes and the manner of my teaching. She was a wonderful teacher, able to encourage academic excellence while allowing incredible fun. As I remembered how helpful she had been to me, the first parent, Barry's mother, arrived for our conference.

Barry was an extremely bright and conscientious young boy. As I looked over the folder of his work that I had prepared, I was sure I was not challenging him to his full potential, and I expected to be told so. I took a deep breath, smiled and invited Barry's mother to take a seat across from me.

Her first words to me were, "Thank you." I know the stunned look on my face prompted her to go on. "I'm sure you don't know this," she said, "but during Barry's first five years of school, he complained of a stomach ache every morning. He begged to stay home and often cried before leaving the house for school. When I spoke with his teachers about it, they had no answers."

"Then this year," she continued, "for the first time since Barry started school, all of that stopped. He got up in the morning and felt fine. He was happy and eager to get to school. When I asked him why he had changed, Barry said that school was fun now. He said that you were nice and that you don't yell. You joke and laugh in class, and he is not afraid to make a mistake. Barry said he's not afraid of school anymore."

As I drifted off to sleep later that night, I thought about how powerful the words of Barry's mother were. "Barry said that he is no longer afraid in school."

## A Moment: Nicki and the Principal's Office

Nicki sat down on the brown vinyl chair in the principal's outer office, and I sat beside her. The principal came out of her main office when she learned we were waiting to see her and pulled up a chair across from us.

"I brought Nicki down here to see you," I said, "because everything I've tried doesn't seem to be helping and, frankly, I don't know what else to do. I am particularly concerned because Nicki is not doing her work; she is often tardy, and she is very disruptive during class. I have tried a number of things to help her, but nothing seems to work. I'm hoping you can give us some suggestions."

Before I could continue—about how I thought Nicki and I needed some assistance in communicating clearly, even though Nicki seemed to be trying—the principal interrupted me with a long list of unacceptable behaviours she wanted Nicki to change "or else." Her list included things Nicki had done from years past as well as a list of complaints from other teachers. In the background, the steam radiator hissed as the principal rattled off Nicki's vices, her voice louder and louder. Meanwhile, Nicki's head dropped lower and lower. I could not listen anymore. What had I done? At the first pause, I quickly stood up.

"Come on, Nicki, or we'll miss English class," I said, gently touching her on the shoulder.

Nicki and I walked silently down the school hall toward the classroom. Just before we reached the classroom door, I turned to her and said, "I'm sorry; I never meant for that to happen."

I was never quite sure what Nicki's nod back to me meant. I do know that I promised myself that I would never do that again. I would figure out other ways to handle difficulties with a student on my own, without asking someone else to take care of conflicts for me. It was an important lesson for my first year of teaching, one that both haunted and helped me in the years that would follow.

**A Moment: Discovering Why**

Several years ago I answered the telephone and was greeted by, "Guess who this is?"

"Can you give me a hint," I asked the young man on the other end of the phone?

"You taught me in school," he replied.

I had taught hundreds of young people since 1973.

"Give me another hint," I pleaded.

"You taught me in sixth grade," he answered.

That was my first year of teaching, and although his voice jarred an image deep in my memory, I couldn't bring his name to the surface. I was silent while I tried to figure out who he was when, all of a sudden, he blurted out the initials to his name. With that hint, I immediately said his name. Ted was pleased that I remembered him. We talked for a long while about what he was doing.

Ted was now 34-years-old. He shared many of the difficulties he had experienced in his life, but assured me that he was doing well now.

"I've been seeing a counsellor for a number of years and it has really helped me to deal with many of the issues in my life that caused me to experience times of depression. I had a lot of anger and pain that I had to deal with as fallout from my family situation as well as from my school days," he shared.

I knew some of what Ted was talking about. He had suffered an incredible amount of teasing from the other students, particularly the boys.

"The continued fear of being humiliated daily by other students coupled with the difficulties that I experienced at home made me dread attending school. I was always the object of so much teasing from other students. They often called me 'fag' or whispered 'get out you little faggot' as I walked by," Ted told me.

He shared this with such emotion that it seemed like it had happened just yesterday. As Ted spoke, I recalled that at times some of the teachers mentioned in the faculty room that they thought Ted acted gay. The remark was usually followed by some laughter. I regret that, because of my own lack of awareness and naiveté, I never addressed the name calling from the students nor the faculty members' remarks. Their remarks and laughter, as I later came to realize, were sexist and reflected deeply homophobic attitudes.

During our conversation, Ted asked me, "Do you remember how I often put my head down on my desk and slept during the first part of the morning?"

"Yes," I said. The memory of the first time that it happened surfaced without much effort.

I was checking attendance in homeroom that morning, and when I called out Ted's name, he didn't answer. Ted's head was down on his desk, and I thought he was playing around. I called out his name a second time only this time a little louder. I walked over to his desk and called his name a third time. He never lifted his head. At first I wasn't sure what to do. I stood there for a minute and then touched his shoulder and called his name until he awakened.

"Ted, are you sick?"

A barely audible "No" was his reply.

"Then why are you asleep?"

"I didn't sleep most of the night and I'm very tired," he said hesitantly.

I was torn over what to do. If I let him sleep, would I relinquish my control of the class? While I occasionally felt like the class got out of control, most of the time there was some semblance of order in the room. If I let students begin to put their heads down and sleep in class, what would it lead to? How would I look? It was difficult enough being a first-year teacher. All of the group work we did in language arts, social studies, and English, as well as the art, music, and physical education made maintaining order difficult. What would this bring? Would they all try to go to sleep? Just as I was about to say to him that he had to stay awake for class, I looked at his face and saw the dark circles under his eyes and the fearful look within them.

"Go ahead and sleep for a while," I said and smiled just enough so that he knew that it was all right. Ted put his head down on the desk and fell back to sleep.

After school that day Ted waited in the classroom to talk. He thanked me for not yelling at him for falling asleep and then proceeded to share with me why he was so exhausted. His father would often come home very late at night after he was out drinking. His mother would be very upset and they would usually get into a fierce argument. Ted would awaken to the sound of his parents screaming at one another in the middle of the night. He was so afraid and upset that he was unable to fall back to sleep. When his alarm went off in the morning, he would get up and get ready for school totally exhausted from lack of sleep. All of this had happened again last night. He said previous teachers had yelled at him for putting his head down and falling asleep. Some told him that he was lazy, while others reprimanded him for staying up too late at night and watching television. Ted said that I was the first teacher who ever came over to his desk and asked him why.

**Author Contemplation: Faith in Classroom Relationships**

When I look back at these moments with Barry, Nicki, and Ted, complicated feelings and self-images invite me to examine how differently I responded and how I might better understand the teacher/student relationship. For Barry and Ted, I had created a space in the classroom where they felt safe and affirmed through interacting in very real and human ways. Because Nicki had low grades, broke rules, and was not doing her work, I justified taking her to the principal on the premise of helping her academically.

When I realized that I had placed Nicki in a situation where her already minimal self-worth was exposed to further diminishment, I was forced to probe the merit of my action and vowed I would never knowingly do that to a student again. My different ways of interacting with Barry and Nicki represented a choice I would have to make about what kind of learner/teacher relationship I valued. I could not give credence to both paradigms as I came to see them as more and more incompatible. One paradigm is rooted in an ideology of what James Macdonald (1995) calls achievement. The other paradigm views the learner/teacher relationship as grounded in faith.

Faith, although often associated with religion, can also be viewed in a much wider sense as the core of connection in human relationships. According to the *Oxford English Dictionary* (Simpson & Weiner, 1989), the principle senses of faith are a trust and belief in someone or something. Additionally, faith yields confidence and engagement. Faith, as the core of connection in human relationships, involves acts of trust that risk placing my belief in someone or something beyond myself. Faith yields the belief that something is possible beyond what I can know, prove or even describe both within myself and in another. Infinite possibilities come to light in placing my life in relationship to another in faith, yet a great deal of fragility is also present within this exchange because faith is intricately linked to human freedom.

The human dimensions of faith as linked to human freedom have been given some of its clearest expression within the discourses of liberation theology. In response to the question, "What is faith?" comes the perception from one black liberation theologian that "it is a contextual faith which comes out of the commitment to the struggle" and "is born in the womb of the struggle itself" (Goba, 1990, p. 22). For Goba, faith is "deprivatized...communal...calls for resistance in any situation of oppression and dehumanization...and the central axis which shapes and directs every aspect of life (23–25)." In this sense, faith is not an individual act of assent to a body of hidden truths, but rather faith is coming to see what was previously unseen about the reality of our shared lives.

In a similar way, learners and teachers express a relationship based on faith not through articulation of formal doctrines, but rather through openness to contextual and experiential meaning and trust in ordinary, day-to-day exchanges. When relationships between teachers and learners—and learners and learners—are rooted in faith, being and learning together becomes less about individual achievement and more about the communal shaping and sharing of knowledge that benefits everyone. Relationships rooted in faith call us to support those among us who suffer most from forms of oppression—such as can be found in tracking and grading—and to resist the dehumanizing effects of schooling manifested in prescriptive and pre-packaged curriculum, high-stakes testing, rigid control and strict codes of discipline.

*Etymology of Faith*

Etymologically, faith can be traced to the Greek word *pistij*, the Latin *fides* and later, the Middle English *feith*.

Educational relationships rooted in faith defy expression in the technical language of behavioural objectives and student measurement embedded in the ideology of achievement. Macdonald (1995) describes the ideology of achievement in the following manner:

> It is the rhetoric of behaviorism, scientism, and psychologism. People are "learners," who have to be "motivated" and "measured," and who possess certain "traits," "capacities," and "needs" which we "diagnose." Goals are talked about in "behavioral" terms. This rhetoric has the effect of lifting the burden of our moral responsibility to children (and other people). It creates a mystique about schooling into which one must be initiated through a teacher education program and the rite of certification, and it creates a jargon which obscures our fundamental moral concern.

Thus, it becomes easy to keep our focus upon the achievement of learning goals and to forget the fundamental goal of freeing persons for self-responsible and self-directed fulfillment of their own emerging potential. It is easy to talk about norms, percentiles, concepts, skills, methods, and so forth; and it is equally as easy to forget about the person involved. (52)

Diane Ravitch (2010), once an advocate for standardized testing, has now become a strong critic of such a narrow form of achievement. She states: "Testing, I realized with dismay, had become a central preoccupation in the schools and was not just a measure but an end in itself. I came to believe that accountability, as written into federal law, was not raising standards but dumbing down the schools as states and districts strived to meet unrealistic targets (p. 12)." A relationship based on faith invites us to risk seeing the other person in fresh and new ways, to believe that the possibility for growth is always present in the other person and within oneself. Relationships grounded in faith actuate a human response to students and peers within the school setting.

Often without realizing it, acts of faith are exchanged between a teacher and a student through a way of being. In the article, "The Closed and Open Contract: Two Irreconcilable Structures in the Curriculum," Garman (1990) suggests:

The teacher and learner are involved in a unique experience where educators can shape the involvements where events have special meanings and where actions are significant because they are part of a larger action. Schooling implies that all participants "encounter" learning in contrived ways. Tradition as well as technique guides the action, and nonrational forces such as faith and caring are as important as appropriate behavioral intervention methods and materials for the success of the encounters. The teaching/learning relationship has explicit and implicit assumptions concerning its nature and complexity. (p. 178)

Although I was not conscious of it at the time, my encounter with Ted was guided by a force of faith. Our interaction was a witness to the power of what can happen when the dignity of the other person is primary and respect is shown through the freedom of personal choice. This form of exchange in faith is contrary to prescriptive, technical, punitive and authoritarian models of discipline that are often valued in schools. A relationship between teacher and learner rooted in faith is not something obtained in the prescriptive how-to approaches of classroom and behaviour management. Issues of discipline and punishment are intricately linked to issues of power and the locus of control in the classroom.

I thought about the ways that the notion of discipline is conceived in schooling. Humiliation, authoritarianism, rewards, punishment, guilt, and control are viewed as ways to keep order. Many unjust actions are committed in schools and yet justified in the name of discipline, order and control. Donald S. Blumenfeld-Jones (1996) argues that

> Classroom discipline systems are, in particular, moral systems in that "all ethical systems are relational; that is, all ethical theories say something about how moral agents should relate to external entities" (Noddings, 1989, p. 183). In schools these external entities are the various constituencies with which students interact (administrators, teachers, staff, fellow students, visitors) as well as the rules and regulations which are presented as symbols of underlying moral principles. While experiencing disciplinary activities, students emerge with a strong sense of who they are in relation to society and what they can expect from that. In other words, students are educated, through these systems, to a particular moral stance. (pp. 5-6)

Blumenfeld-Jones offers a critique of three discipline systems used in schools—Assertive Discipline, Glasser's Control Theory, and Discipline with Dignity. All are "patriarchal moral systems focused on hyper-individuality and dependent upon rules, consequences, and principles focused through authoritarian structures." He proposes freedom of (not from) responsibility as an "alternative grounding" (p. 5). Drawing from the work of Noddings, Welch, and Buber to explicate this concept, Blumenfeld-Jones comments:

Freedom of responsibility means the ability to respond to being in communion, being opened up and drawn in to others, recognizing our fundamental dependence on others and the interdependence among all. (p. 20)

Classroom relationships shaped by faith enhance the potential for discipline grounded in freedom of responsibility to emerge rather than the "conventional classroom discipline through which the patriarchy speaks" (p. 20). Codes of discipline, demerits, detentions, and other disciplinary action may get young persons to behave in the way we want. Nonetheless, all of this falls very short of touching the human spirit and encouraging a person to grow. Life is filled with uncertainty and chaos, yet there is a powerful testimony of faith that expresses a belief in the unseen reality that persons can grow and change when love and respect are shown. A pedagogy of faith is in contrast to a pedagogy of achievement. Demonstrations of control may yield desired behaviour, but in the process, human freedom is denied.

In my current university position, particularly in classes with pre-service teachers, I try to live out the lessons that Barry, Nicki Ted had shown me. It is not always easy to respond from the belief of *freedom of responsibility*. It is often difficult to find the time needed for both myself and the persons in the class to come to an awareness of our failings, to create the space for forgiveness and reconciliation, and to live in such a way that a group of individuals could be transformed into a compassionate and loving community of learners. It is challenging to share power with learners as opposed to exercising power over (Kreisberg, 1992) them. Approaching classroom situations in a relational manner, while difficult, can create opportunities for a pedagogy of faith and "freedom of responsibility" as a basis of choice in the classroom to emerge. This can and should happen at any and every level of education.

## Student Contemplations on Faith in Classroom Relationships

*Student Contemplation on Faith in Classroom Relationships #1*

*On the Notion of Faith in Classroom Relationships: A Meditation* gave me a very insightful view into several issues that I am currently struggling with. Can I meet the educational needs of my students? Do I have the patience and compassion for children that seem they can't be taught? Whenever someone asks me why I decided to go into education in my mid-30s, I often give the joking response that I want to teach kids what not to do. Having done it all myself and traveling down many dead end roads in my life, I found lately that the person I had the least amount of faith in was myself.

This article helped me realize that the answer to some of the above questions is "yes." In fact I now believe that I am more than qualified. To me teaching is much more than the classic saying, "Reading, Writing and Arithmetic". Education is giving children the tools they need for survival in this ever growing problematic world. I am convinced that if my teachers had spent more time teaching me life skills, and less time trying to control my behavior, then maybe, just maybe I would have had the self-discipline to learn the educational basics. Without these life and self-discipline skills, even the simple basics can seem overwhelming to a child. This can make the learning environment a scary and foreign place, making the child just want to run and hide.

Of course I can't blame all my trials in life on my teachers. However thinking back on my educational experiences, I can't think of one teacher until my senior year of high school who tried to relate to me and foster my ideas. I can't help now but to feel a little cheated. I want my future students to have faith in me. I want to help them with their personal issues and dilemmas and make them the best possible people they can be. No child, whether from the most elite of neighborhoods or from the inner-city has a chance unless they believe in him or herself. As a teacher, I have to believe in my students. I have to have faith in their abilities; if I don't, who will? Unfortunately, you cannot presume that anyone will. You can't assume that they will get this type of encouragement.

Reading, writing, and arithmetic will be comprehended if and only if the student believes in him/herself. Take it from a person who passed every grade between first and twelfth grades with little room to spare. Take it from someone who was told by his guidance counselor to figure out something else other than pursuing a college education. It's hard to believe in yourself when no one believes in you. I have to ask myself what kind of teacher I want to be. One who fosters growth or one who prevents it? Fostering growth seems much more rewarding. If that means having faith in the child no one believes in, I dare anyone to check my student success rate in thirty years.

*Student Contemplation on Faith in Classroom Relationships #2*

I was able to see faith as more than just a religious term. Different examples in the article exemplify how teachers may address a variety of classroom issues and make a difference, and ultimately respect the worth and dignity of students. Beginning teachers may face many challenges and find they are using conflicting paradigms in different situations. For example, with Barry, a paradigm that viewed the learner/teacher relationship as one grounded in faith was used. However, the same teacher used a paradigm based on the ideology of achievement when dealing with Nicki. Barry was left feeling good and unafraid because the faith paradigm allowed the teacher and learner to make a connection. Barry trusted and believed in his teacher. Nicki on the other hand was left with diminished self-worth. Faith is fragile and involves engagement, community, respect, belief, and trust. In education, faith allows relationships to be built on something more than behavioral objectives and grading scales.

I was really touched by the story of Ted. I wonder how I would react in such a situation. I hope I would (I think that the story will help me to) try to act similarly in a difficult situation. It is this kind of story that helps future teachers look beyond academics and remember to think about the why of student behavior. Students have much more going on than just school and we need to keep this in mind. Educational relationships that are built on faith are much more likely to have positive outcomes for both students and teachers.

I was able to see what faith can really mean and the effects it can have. I always thought of faith as a religious term and nothing else. However, I now see that faith is more than that. By building relationships grounded in faith, teachers and students are able to gain dignity and respect that go beyond the classroom walls. It is so important for students to have positive relationships with adults so that they can feel safe and comfortable. Teachers need to provide this because students may not get it elsewhere. Faith can help us do this because it encompasses all of the positive aspects of a relationship such as mutual trust and respect, dignity, belief and understanding.

*Student Contemplation on Faith in Classroom Relationships #3*

As a future educator I feel that the notion of faith in the classroom can be extremely helpful to both the educator and the learner. As a student I always feared making a mistake in school or doing the wrong thing. Often I would just sit back silently, hoping my fellow classmates would answer the questions being posed. I was worried I would answer incorrectly or not understand the question. As I grew up I began to think of school as a number system. It was based on letter grades and points. There was never a real concern with my opinion, feelings or learning. I was just another student that was expected to listen, and maintain high scores.

I believe that having relationships rooted in faith can help me to prevent situations similar to what I experienced as a student. I feel that if I am not willing to believe in each and every one of my students, how can I expect those students to believe in anything I say or do? I feel if my students and I have faith in each other, there will be greater confidence in one another. Students will be more willing to try new things, share their ideas, and make mistakes.

I believe that everyone continues to grow, no matter what their age. It is crucial that as educators we allow our students to feel the support and strength behind them. A teacher-student, teacher-teacher, or student-student relationship rooted in faith allows for that growth to continue to take place. We will begin to see each other in new ways and feel the courage that each individual needs, and continue to use that to strengthen our relationships.

*Student Contemplation on Faith in Classroom Relationships #4*

I really liked the following sentence in the article, "demonstrations of control may yield desired behavior, but in the process human freedom is denied." I think that this is an important point that a lot of teachers may forget. When teachers call out students in front of the class, it is embarrassing for that student. And after that the student may get scared or just not show any interest because they do not care anymore. They feel as though they are not respected within the classroom.

*Student Contemplation on Faith in Classroom Relationships #5*

After reading *On the Notion of Faith in Classroom Relationships* my mind hooks into the concept of teaching as a commitment to the struggle. It is through the context of the struggle that faith manifests—in oneself as a compassionate human being first and then as a teacher, and in one's students as bearers of unseen potentials.

I agree that faith is a relational exchange between all learners in the classroom; however, it is the teacher who holds the space to expand or contract that struggle, and consequently the outcomes. Judaism is dedicated to *tikun alom*, (repairing the world) and *gemilut chasadim* (loving kindness), which I believe complements this discussion. Repairing the world, one student at a time, is what a teacher sets out to do, and loving kindness is the influential container within which these relationships are held.

As a teacher I will choose to follow the face of the rightness of things, even when they do not seem right—such as when Ted put his head on his desk and the teacher wrestles with the decision to let him sleep. Where does this decision come from? The teacher takes a 'risk seeing the other person in fresh and new ways' and her response is a 'human response.' Ted is perceived compassionately as an individual with needs, albeit unseen, which calls for a 'belief in unseen reality.' This is human faith of epic proportions, which translates into respect and dignity, something we all need, particularly vulnerable children in our classrooms.

Freedom of responsibility requires a respectful relationship between teacher and student hopefully resulting in trust and the elevation of human beings. Many students arrive at school with a myriad of cognitive, social and emotional needs with an underlying relational hunger—which results in poor choices and decisions. A presence of faith between teacher and student has the potential to satisfy this hunger and open avenues for students to trust themselves, thus creating positive events in their lives.

I am committed to teaching and the struggle of repairing the world. I humbly look forward to future student relationships and how they will influence my faith in the unseen.

*Student Contemplation on Faith in Classroom Relationships #6*

The article, *On the Notion of Faith in Classroom Relations*, discusses what it means to have a connection of faith with your students. This kind of faith that Llewellyn talks about is the kind in which she makes a deeper connection with her students. This enables her to understand her students more and for her students to respect her more. Llewellyn gives some examples of these connections she has made. She talks about her early years of teaching and reflects on the experiences she had with some of her students.

One of the first things Llewellyn discusses is the anxiety she felt right before her first parent/teacher conference. She thought the child's parents were going to ask her questions about why she was not challenging their son more. However, the parents thanked her because for the first time, their son enjoys school. Llewellyn provided a safe environment for her students so they can feel comfortable in the classroom. She tried to make her lessons creative and engaging for her students. She also tried to understand her students. Ted, one of her students, would always fall asleep in homeroom. Instead of yelling at him, Llewellyn asked him why he is so tired. Ted said it was the first time anyone has ever asked that and said it was because his parents fight at night. Instead of making Ted follow the rules, she let him sleep until class started. Another child Llewellyn talks about is Nicki. When Nicki was acting out, Llewellyn took her to the office, where the principal yelled at her and put her down for the many negative things she had done. Llewellyn felt that only made matters worse. This brings me to the next insight of the article, which is handling situations in your own way. Llewellyn felt the principal handled that situation in a wrong way and promised herself that in the future she would handle discipline herself. I think for a beginning teacher, figuring out how to discipline your students can be difficult. It is important to figure out how you want to go about handling situations in the classroom. I like how Llewellyn is more concerned about the students and not the discipline of the students.

Llewellyn relates her experiences to her beliefs as a teacher, which brings me to my last insight. She talks about the importance of faith, or believing in her students no matter what. I really like how she ended the article talking about how being strict with your students may produce the wanted behaviors and grades. However, being compassionate, forgiving, and caring will help students grow as individuals.

As teachers, I think we all will say that we are compassionate and caring, but are we forgiving? I think forgiveness is the most important thing in life. Students should be able to have some sort of freedom in the classroom. Having control in a classroom is important; however, what's the point if the control takes away so much freedom that the students are afraid to be in school? Students need to be able to feel comfortable so they have room to grow. Teachers need to have a classroom practice that allows for this growth.

*Student Contemplation on Faith in Classroom Relationships #7*

The Story of Ted is one that I can relate too. I was teased throughout school for as far back as I can remember which is about third grade. There were a few things that happened to me. There were times that I wished that my teacher and other students would have stepped in and helped with the teasing but they never did. Still to this day I wonder why no one did. Students would say the same things to me "fag" or "why are you in our school?" When I would tell the teacher or principal what they said, they would say, "You need to change the way you act. It is your fault that they are teasing you." I always felt that I did not need to change, they did, because they were in the wrong, not me. I feel that this is why it took me so many years to admit that I was gay. I tried for years to fit in with the way that Christians and society wanted me to be. It always felt wrong and I felt that I was lying to myself for not being who I really am as a human being. I hated going to school. I dreaded every day of the twelve years. I missed the maximum days allowed so that l would not have to put up with the teasing, threats of physical harm, and the sexual innuendoes from other boys during gym class. I hated that class the most. My teachers probably talked and gossiped about my sexual orientation in the teacher's lounge. Looking back on all of this, I should have dropped out of school. I had faith that one day it would be better for later generations than it was for me. I knew that God created me this way for a reason and that one day he would reveal that to me.

I plan to have faith in my students and build a relationship that is based on a faith that invites all of us to risk seeing people in fresh new ways. We will all have to believe that growth is possible and that it is always present in every one that we meet. By doing this I will show my student that relationships that have faith actuate a response for caring, nurturing and trusting in the school setting.

*Student Contemplation on Faith in Classroom Relationships #8*

I place high value on student and teacher relationships. This type of relationship is a bond; it's a commitment. It's almost like a marriage. You can't see the bond and you can't express in words what the bond is like. All you can do is show people that it's there. I want to make sure that I form some type of bond with each and every one of my students. As I read *On the Notion of Faith in Classroom Relationships: A Meditation,* I saw how hard we as humans can be on ourselves. The story of Nicki reminded me of an experience I had not too long ago. I work for an extended day program. Each school has a before and after school program right at the school. However, this program is not through the school, it's a non-profit organization. The principal is the boss, but not really. One day two of the 5th graders didn't want to wait until the bell rang for me to dismiss them to leave. They said they were leaving to go to school. I told them that if they left I'd go to the principal. Now I knew inside I wasn't going to go to the principal. I didn't want him to have to deal with my problems and I didn't want to look weak. At the same time I wanted these boys to get into trouble for leaving before the bell rang. I did the same thing as you; I told myself I can't do this ever again. I decided to create stronger relationships with these two boys so that they'd want to listen to me. I feel as if I did rely on faith to help me. I lost the battle between the kids and I didn't want this to happen again. I had to look past this incident and move on. I can't dislike these kids because they didn't listen to me. My faith keeps me moving forwards. I don't think teachers and students are aware of the fact that relationships are built upon faith. Faith and bonds allow us to listen and react to different issues, just like the discussion between you and Ted. I know that there will be happy and sad experiences. I know good and bad experiences will happen too. My faith is what will help me decide what to do next.

*Student Contemplation on Faith in Classroom Relationships #9*

An idea that I thought was important was that when relationships between teachers and learners and learners and learners are rooted in faith being and learning together becomes less about the individual person and more about the community sharing and molding knowledge that benefits everyone. This is a very profound idea that if used by more teachers would result in more classrooms that are communities of learners where all ideas and opinions are valued. If the students and teachers feel that they have a strong and trusting relationship then everyone will feel comfortable expressing themselves and asking for help if they need it. Also, this situation makes the learning feel more like a conversation between teachers and students and among students instead of a teacher standing in front of the room talking to the students while they listen without giving any feedback. Going along with this is that if a relationship is based on faith, it invites people including teachers and students to see each other in a fresh way. That means that the possibility of growth is always there in them and that they will see each other for who they really are not simply a student who cannot behave or a teacher who tells their students what they can and cannot do. Teachers will see students as children who are all different and "smart" in their own way while students will see their teacher as a caring person who wants them to succeed in life.

A final idea that I felt was important was that rewards for achievement and good grades may motivate students to learn factual information and spit it back out for assignments. However, none of these things touch the human spirit encouraging a person to grow like knowing someone has faith in you. I feel that if a student feels that no one has faith in them, they will lose faith in themselves and give up. When I have my own classroom, I will have to foster a relationship of faith and trust with all of my students and colleagues.

*Student Contemplation on Faith in Classroom Relationships #10*

After reading the article, *On the Notion of Faith in Classroom Relationships: A Meditation*, there were several things that really struck me. I really loved reading about Barry. I am sure it must have felt incredibly rewarding to hear that Barry loved coming to school because he was no longer afraid, and because he was having fun. I admire the way in which you conducted your classes and treated your students. School should be a place where students feel safe and happy, and there should be smiles and laughter in every classroom. The scenario with Barry is a prime example of how teachers can make such an impact on the lives of their students, and how truly amazing and rewarding the teaching profession is and can be. As a future educator, I am looking forward to creating a fun and exciting classroom environment. I want my students to want to come to school, just as Barry did. I want my students to experience joy and laughter, and I do not want them to ever be afraid of coming into my classroom. I felt that the situation with Ted was another powerful, yet rewarding teaching experience. The situation displays why it is so critical for teachers to know their students, and to take interest in their students' lives. I felt that you made an excellent judgment call by allowing Ted to sleep at his desk. As teachers, we may never know what exactly is going on in our students' lives, but it is extremely important that we pay attention to our students' actions and/or feelings. Teachers have the power to be so many different figures in a child's life: an educator, a mentor, a role model, and a friend; therefore, teachers should take advantage of these different roles and try to make a difference in their students' lives. This situation definitely reflected a relationship rooted in faith between a teacher and learner because the teacher saw the student suffering and instead of forcing the student to participate, the teacher supported the student's needs. I truly admire that you acknowledged Ted as a person, rather than just another student. I also really admire the way in which you acknowledged Nicki as a person, as well. I think many teachers would have reacted the same way if they were dealing with a student who was not doing his/her work, and who was breaking the rules. Too often, teachers jump the gun and discipline students without realizing that disciplining the student may actually be making the situation worse. I learned by reading this article how important it is to create relationships based on faith, rather than achievement. As a future teacher, I will be more aware of creating faith based relationships with my students.

*Student Contemplation on Faith in Classroom Relationships #11*

I never related faith as an important factor of relationships with students, until I read this article. I strongly believe that teachers must first build relationships that obtain trust and belief in a person. I feel that relationships come first in a classroom, even before academics and management. Students need to feel a bond between themselves and their teacher. Although, I am only a classroom assistant right now, each day I take the time necessary to build a relationship with all of the first grade students. I notice how the students respond differently to me as opposed to a teacher who abides by a strong disciplinary classroom.

Reading this article was very beneficial. I found myself relating to this article and all of its significant points. As a teacher, I plan to use faith to enhance the relationships amongst my students and me. I feel that any teacher who has a positive relationship with all students can have a classroom with management, without the discipline.

*Student Contemplation on Faith in Classroom Relationships #12*

I hope to create a classroom environment based on the pedagogy of faith. This pedagogy, where the student is a human being who has the capability of growth in ways that may be unimaginable if only he or she is nurtured, encouraged, and advocated for, is what I want my students to learn. Based on my own school experiences, learning does not consist of memorizing facts to spew onto a test. True learning is experiencing and caring about knowledge gained; the type of learning you can take with you for the rest of your life not only academically but socially, culturally, emotionally. Focusing "less about individual achievement and more about the communal shaping and sharing of knowledge" will teach students wisdom that far surpasses the knowledge of how to take a test.

Society is intricate. We expect members of our society to be accomplished in so many ways, yet narrowly focus on one way of teaching that is driven by testing standards. Teaching cannot be administering facts, because we will be doing our students a costly injustice. The classroom must be a place where your students believe in you and you in them. Faith involves the ability to trust that together you can accomplish and succeed, grow and continue growth.

I want to create a community where my students feel safe to ask questions, make mistakes, and learn from each other. I want my students to trust me with their minds, feelings, and attitudes. I want my classroom to birth relationships and open-minds. This all starts with a faith that this environment is absolutely possible. I will have faith in my students—a secure belief that they will succeed and accomplish each expectation I have for them. I also sincerely hope that my students will have faith in me to help them make a transformation in their lives.

*Student Contemplation on Faith in Classroom Relationships #13*

*On the Notion of Faith in Classroom Relationships: A Meditation* was certainly the best article I have read for this course thus far. I was easily able to relate to the practical real-life examples, and I have been inspired to maintain quality relationships within my future classroom(s). Although the article's primary focus was not the feelings surrounding a teacher's first few years, I feel that I benefitted from learning that a "real" teacher struggled to find ways to make the material interesting while also maintaining order and control in the classroom, as these are aspects of becoming a teacher that worry me. I am also relieved to know that not all teachers refuse to smile before Christmas. I want my students to feel comfortable and at home in the classroom, which would be difficult if there were no smiling and joking.

    The short story of the major change is Barry's attitude towards school was inspiring. I am not becoming a teacher because I want to fill children's minds with massive amounts of information. I am becoming a teacher because I want to form relationships with my students that nurture within them a passion for learning. My hope is that I can touch children like Barry and make a difference in children's lives. That is why I want to be a teacher.

    The part of the article about Nicki reinforced what many of my professors are currently telling me. I need to handle my own discipline issues within the classroom. I cannot and should not send my students to the office unless the issue is one of student or personal safety. The comparison of the differences in the interactions between Barry and Nicki encouraged me to think about what I will prioritize when forming these future relationships with my students. Will it be academic achievement or faith? It is often the case where the students who are intelligent receive the most (positive) attention. How unfair is it to focus my attention on the students most unlike Nikki and Barry? Had the author of the article chosen pure academic achievement alone, both of these relationships would have failed. Nicki and Barry needed just that one teacher to believe in them.

What about Ted? Most teachers would have sent the child to the nurse, the office, or reprimanded him in some way for deliberately sleeping in class. By prioritizing faith and compassion over control and academics, the author was able to take the first steps in forming a much needed relationship with Ted. I want to be the teacher upon whom students can rely. I want to be the teacher that chooses faith, kindness, and compassion over academic achievement because I believe that prioritizing one will bring the other. I want to be the teacher who follows her heart. I want to be the teacher that changes lives, or at least makes a lasting impact.

*Student Contemplation on Faith in Classroom Relationships #14*

I could not stop reading the article *On the Notion of Faith in Classroom Relations*. One thing that kept sticking in my mind is the different students and the different personalities in the classroom. It is hard for us to imagine our first classroom as anything but perfect. But this article shows us two students who are totally different with different abilities. This kept sticking out to me because I sometimes forget how different students are. I think back when I was in school and if the teacher would have just taken some time to teach because I learned differently maybe things would have come to me a little more easily rather than me struggling all through school.

Another idea that stuck out to me while reading this article and even after was how scared the author was. She felt scared and nervous and she admits to her mistakes throughout the article. We often forget that it is alright for us to make mistakes and be scared. Teaching is scary and we are often going to feel nervous teaching twenty totally different students. It was a relief to read someone with a lot of experience feels scared and able to admit mistakes. We are bound to make mistakes but it's what we learn from our mistakes that are important.

Everyone likes to have a relationship and feel that bond with someone. In the article it shows us that children are no different. Children are with us for at least eight hours a day, five days a week. Having a bond with each and every one of our students is critical. Both teachers and students need to have faith in the relationship in the classroom. Having this kind of faith in a relationship is seeing growth in the other person. When we have a relationship with someone, we see things that we do not usually see. When you ask a person to talk about a teacher that they remember previously most likely people are going to name the teachers that they had developed a relationship with. Some students go through bullying, problems at home, emotional problems, and many other pressures and difficulties. The one thing that students need to be able to rely on is the relationship they have with you and the faith they have in your relationship. Students need to know that they can rely on your relationship and know that they can trust in you.

Everybody wants to feel like they have a relationship with someone. Having a bond with someone makes you see the other person in a different way. Not only will you see growth in your students after developing a bond but you will also see a growth in yourself.

*Chapter 4*

# Contemplation on a Praxis of Compassion

## A Moment: John and the First Day of School

It was the first day of school, and John arrived just before the bell rang. The terror at the prospect of being in school was so clearly visible on his face that it was chilling to see. Despite his fear and resistance, John was required to stay at school. The teacher welcomed him warmly at the 1st grade classroom door and attempted to make John feel safe and welcomed. All efforts to comfort him, however, seemed to fail. The young boy timidly made his way to a self-selected space beneath the teacher's tan metal desk where he remained for the entire day.

The following morning John was forced to return to school. Once again he made his way to the spot beneath the teacher's desk. Day after day, John returned to that place beneath the desk. Sometimes he wept to the point of making himself physically sick. One day the teacher brought a blanket, a pillow and a flashlight and handed them to John. He took the blanket and laid it out carefully under the desk. John then propped the pillow against the inside of the desk and leaned against it as he explored a children's book by the light of the flashlight.

John remained under the teacher's desk for nearly a month. Each day he would carefully lay out the blanket, lean against the pillow and complete his work almost perfectly by flashlight. At one point toward the end of the month, the teacher noticed that John had crept out from beneath the desk and had moved ever so slightly away from the desk. The next day the same thing occurred. However, this time John moved even further away from the tan metal desk and began to inch his way toward the middle of the floor. Each day John made his way closer to an empty desk on the other side of the room until one day he crawled up into his assigned seat.

## A Moment: Mark & the Empty Lot

One morning during my second year as the principal of an urban Catholic elementary school, Mark, a sixth-grade student, did not show up for class. Mark's mother said that he had left for school with his brothers and sisters, but he never arrived. I decided to drive around and look for him. I eventually found him a few blocks away from the school sitting on a cement block in an empty lot. I parked the car and, when I walked over to him, he barely looked up. He just shrugged his shoulders when I asked him what was wrong. I did not try to force him to go back to school, but asked him to get in the car where we could talk better.

Mark agreed and walked with me to the car where we then sat and talked for a while. He spoke mostly about where he went to school before and what he liked and didn't like about school now. After about 20 minutes, I approached him about going to school. When he said that he couldn't, I took him to McDonald's and bought him breakfast. He said very little while he ate, but when he finished, he agreed to go back to school.

The next day he wasn't in homeroom again. I headed to the same empty lot where I had found Mark the previous day. No matter how hard I tried I could not get him to talk about what was wrong. I wasn't sure what to do. I wondered if he was manipulating me. Some parents and faculty members had already criticized me for not being strict enough.

This continued for a few days until finally one morning Mark began to talk about what was bothering him. As he spoke, he began to cry. His father and mother were divorced. His dad lived on the same block, and Mark saw him often. When Mark went to visit his dad earlier that week, he found his dad and another man involved in a horrible fight. When he saw the knife, he ran away and was afraid to tell anyone. He returned to his dad's house a few hours later and saw blood on the floor when he looked through the window, but his dad was not there. Mark was sure that his dad had been killed and blamed himself for running away. He kept going over to his dad's house to see if he was there. He felt that he couldn't stay at school until he found his dad.

I asked Mark to take me to his dad's house. It was as he had described, and I felt sick as I walked away from that window. We spent the rest of the morning with his mother, who contacted a few persons and was eventually able to find Mark's father. His Dad told him that he had been stabbed in a fight, but assured him he was doing well. Mark returned with me to school that afternoon better than he had been a few days before, but certainly not fine. There was a great deal of healing that Mark still needed. It was probably more than we were able to give, yet it seemed important to still try.

**Author Contemplation: A Praxis of Compassion**

What in John's teacher drew her to respond this way to his fear of school? How do I even talk about her response, a response expressed not as a way of acting, a way of behaving, nor a technique, but as a way of being? I imagined myself in her place and wondered if I would have been so compassionate. I spent time in contemplation and entered as fully as I could into this story. What I came to understand is my interpretation. It is reflective of my awareness and not meant to imply that this was how the teacher saw herself in the situation.

The teacher responded to John with her being, and within her being she embodied compassion. She reached out to alleviate John's suffering not through behavioural reinforcements, classroom management techniques, rewards, incentives, or the false promise that everything would be fine. She reached out with her very being in care and compassion and entered into solidarity and shared suffering with John. With no blueprint or script to follow, she relied on intuition to lead her. In *Awakening Intuition*, Frances E. Vaughan (1979) explicates four levels of intuition—physical, emotional, mental, and spiritual. For Vaughan, spiritual intuition consists of ineffable experiences that occur independently of sensation, thought, or feeling. It is an awareness that transcends a personal familiarity and understanding of something. The teacher's response to John is exemplary of such spiritual intuition, what Thomas Merton calls "intuition as an aspect of Being." It was, as John Miller (1994) says in his book, *The Contemplative Practitioner*, an "intuition that moves beyond dualism to experience unity directly" (p. 24).

This teacher brought John a blanket, pillow and flashlight for his physical comfort, but allowed him the freedom to respond to the compassion that she extended by giving him the choice to decide when he was ready to leave the safety of the space under her desk. This teacher's being enabled her to forego all the power issues that sometimes get in the way of a compassionate response. In many ways, John's teacher manifested what Nel Noddings (1995) views as critical characteristics of a person who deeply cares.

> What I found in my own analysis are two characteristics that seem to describe the consciousness of carers in all caring encounters: First, the carer attends to the cared-for in a special way that I have called engrossment. Other writers—Simone Weil and Iris Murdoch, for example—use the word attention. This attention or engrossment is thoroughly receptive; that is, when we really care, we receive what the other person conveys nonselectively. We do not lay on our own structures, nor do we assimilate what the other says as a mere bit of information. We feel what the other is going through. Indeed, Simone Weil said that the implicit question we ask as we attend in this way is, "What are you going through?"
>
> Second, as we receive what is there in the other, we feel our energy flowing toward the other's predicament or project. We want to relieve a burden, activate a dream, share a joy, or clear up confusion. Temporarily, our own projects are put aside; we are caught up by an internal "I must" that pushes us to respond to the other. (p. 67)

Nel Noddings' highly developed work in the phenomenology of caring reflects a growing body of literature in the field of curriculum related to the concept of caring in schools. Noddings' notion of caring as a central element of curriculum in schools is vital. Yet, there is something beyond caring, something else that was revealed in this teacher's response to John. Something called compassion.

The word compassion is derived from the Hebrew word *rahamin* which literally means "trembling womb" (Trible, 1978, pp. 31-59). Etymologically, then, compassion is rooted in the maternal image of the attachment between a mother and child. In this bonding, one being is physically joined to another in an extraordinarily intimate relationship of life flow. Drawing on this image, compassion is about the capacity to enter into the experience of another person's life so fully that it enables me to respond in genuine communion and solidarity to the pain, difficulty, alienation, fragility, weakness, or suffering of another. What is demanded beyond instinctual, sentimental, or pietistic responses is a praxis of compassion. The suffering or pain of the other person is experienced in the here and now with such openness that what flows from my being to the other's being is compassion. Kathleen Brehony's (1996) discussion of the "practice of tonglen, which in Tibetan means 'giving and receiving,'" is illustrative of this compassion.

> Tonglen opens a person to the truth of the suffering of others. It unblocks the heart and allows for the full awareness of the loving, expansive radiance of one's true nature. This compassionate oneness with others bridges the gap of pain and suffering and replaces it with an enlightened understanding of the human experience (pp. 106-107).

It is interesting to consider what it would be like to include the ability to show compassion as one of the requirements for teacher certification. The difficulty, of course, is that compassion is not as easily taught as unit lesson plans or classroom management skills that are grounded in the valued behaviorism of educational practice. A person is guided, invited and drawn into the way of compassion through experiences of compassion or the practice of *tonglen*, not through instruction in behavior modification. While authentic teaching must be about the witness of compassion, it is very difficult to teach this in a system that tends to value assessment, order, competition, interchangeable parts, rewards, punishments, and grades.

When I have shared this meditation with pre-service teachers they often relay that they cannot imagine a teacher interacting with a child like John in this way in the current educational climate. Maxine Greene (1995b) describes imagination "as a means through which we can assemble a coherent world" and says that "imagination is what, above all, makes empathy possible" (p.3). Imagination invites us to enter into reality and creatively transform it. Imagination draws on the senses, the emotions and the intellect as one integrated and whole process. It opens up multiple possibilities of what could be while at the same time calling for attentiveness to what is.

While more and more children come to school troubled, traumatized and suffering, it is crucial that teachers resist assessing a child's difficulties from within a medical model. Within that framework, the child is viewed as ill, in need of treatment and healing. Rather than approaching the child from a perspective of what's wrong with him or her, compassion helps me to see the whole person first and then set out to construct an authentic response. William Ayers (1995) claims that "The first and most fundamental challenge to teachers is to see each learner in as full and complete a way as possible…Teaching at its best is first an act of inquiry, investigation, and research into the lives of children" (pp. 5-6). Compassion is a witness of unconditional love. It is a witness of teaching as a vocation, not merely a job. It is a witness that affirms the value and dignity of each child because of who she or he is, not what she or he academically achieves. The witness of compassion is wedded to justice and requires sacrifice and a willingness to lay open one's life for the sake of the other. It is a witness that demands recognition of our privilege and a sharing of power by striving to turn our exclusiveness into inclusiveness. It is a witness that is willing to accept the suffering that comes from trying to change things. It is a witness that embraces the process of reconciliation over the quick fix of punishment. It is the witness of not only valuing wisdom over status, but risking our privileged positions to stand with those children most in need of freedom. It is the witness of human beings meeting one another in authentic and simple encounters. It is the witness of doing what is right because this is what it means to be human.

I learned from Mark how important it was for me to listen with my heart and respond out of a dimension of intuition. Jim Garrison (2010) speaks of "compassionate listening as a creative spiritual activity. Such listening recognizes the suffering of others in ways that open up possibilities for healing and transformative communication. It calls us out of ourselves to a destiny different from what we previously thought possible, but only if we are willing to abandon present identities and set out on a sometimes dangerous journey whose destination cannot be entirely foreseen" (p. 2763). However, this was not always easy to do as a principal. My way of being a principal was often in conflict with what some faculty members as well as parents wanted. Ironically, the very things that parents had valued in me as a teacher were now being criticized in my role as principal.

Compassion opens me to this stance and allows me to walk in solidarity with the child in his or her experience. In this space, I resist the need to control or offer a quick fix. The teacher who allowed John to remain under the desk for a month must have questioned many times whether her response was adequate. I can still see the image of Mark as he sat frightened and all curled up with his knees pulled up to his chin at the far end of the empty lot. I would like to think that I would have gone back daily for as long as it took. I am not sure that I would have responded out of that level of compassion then. I can only hope that I would be able to do so now.

In many ways young children may be much freer in revealing their needs, pain, and suffering. I think of how guarded the learners in my university classes can be most of the time. They have learned the public/private separation and that school is not the place where some of their suffering can be shared. From time to time the overflow of their pain is revealed, although it is hardly ever directly spoken about unless an invitation is extended.

There is an extensive body of work in curriculum literature that develops the importance of caring as part of the educational direction that is needed in our world today. I am grateful for the ways that this work has broadened the thinking about curriculum and schooling. "The education system provides an excellent opportunity for adults and children to explore and practice the mutuality and reciprocity of respect and caring necessary to sustain human life in this democratic society"(Duhon-Sells, Sells, & Mouton, 1997, p. 3). Caring is critical in growing toward compassion. It is vital that persons who desire to be teachers, as well as teachers who walk into classrooms daily, are encouraged to grow in compassion and create experiences for this compassion to grow among young persons.

**Student Contemplations on a Praxis of Compassion**

*Student Contemplation on a Praxis of Compassion #1*

I feel that this article was the most thought changing article I have read. After reading this, I realized how hard it is for me to view the behaviors of children from a non-medical point of view. I have been drilled since day one in my special education courses to look at diagnoses as the main source of undesired behaviors. It is frightening to me to think that if I had not read this article, that I may have carried that view into my career. I do not want to be a teacher that finds a problem and uses the most up-to-date classroom management techniques to extinguish the behavior. I want to be a teacher that looks into the life of the child to find what is hurting him or her. I want to use compassion to treat the pain that a child feels instead of the more popular intervention. I now want to explore the area of compassion in teaching further thanks to this article.

*Student Contemplation on a Praxis of Compassion #2*

I like the idea that we as teachers need to value our students. We need to really get to know who our students are. They should not be known for their academic achievements or disabilities. Each student is an individual and has his or her own story. We should try to connect to each student individually, not as a whole class. This should definitely be considered when you first encounter the student with a disability. The teacher should not let a disability define who that student is. We should get to know and connect with the student and then make our own assessment about that student. This is a big part of being compassionate towards our students. I think this is one area that schools really need to work on. I was at a school during their transition time and when they placed their students into the next grade they gave them codes (for example BH-behavior problem; E-excellent student; B-below average student; R-reading problems). Once they are coded they are divided up into groups for the next grade. The new teachers get to see the codes and labels that each student has. It is things like this that cause teachers to make assumptions about students. It is hard to show compassion to a student who you already have a mind-set of being a troublemaker or problem student. I would hope that I can prevent this in my classroom. I would like to be that compassionate teacher that brings the flashlight to the student that hides under the desk.

*Student Contemplation on a Praxis of Compassion #3*

I can remember my first grade teacher because of the compassion she showed me. Due to the fact that my mother left me, I constantly struggled with going to school every day thinking my grandmother would do the same. My first grade teacher worked with me day after day taking me aside to a quiet area away from the kids where I could still be involved in the lesson, but without others staring at me. If I was having an extra hard day, she would take extra time to work with me while the other children were out at recess until finally I was able to work in my desk like the other children. A little compassion goes a long way.

*Student Contemplation on a Praxis of Compassion #4*

The article, *A Praxis of Compassion: A Meditation* opened my eyes to realize that there is a difference in caring for someone and showing compassion towards that person. The beginning of the article captured my attention and made me question how I would have handled a student like John in my classroom. I do not believe I would have been able to sit back and watch a child hide underneath the teacher's desk for one day, let alone an entire month. The example of compassion made me question the way I would approach children who are not comfortable and do not want to be a part of the community of learners within the classroom.

Unlike many other occupations and jobs, there is not a blueprint or script that a teacher can pull out and review on how to handle many situations in the classroom. Good teachers are ones who care for their students' academic, emotional and social success. Great teachers are the ones who moved beyond caring and have true compassion for their students. To show compassion to students is not something that can be taught in a college classroom to future teachers. It is within an individual.

Teachers are sometimes forced to seek only parts of children. Many people, including teachers, resort to a medical diagnosis for children who are misbehaving. Yet, if someone would take the time to look at the child as a whole human being, it is possible to find a different response to the situation than to just label the student.

Showing compassion towards a person is not an easy task. Teachers have to be willing to put aside their own biases and feelings to reach the lives of their students. As a future teacher, this concept worries me. Children can be just as complicated as adults, yet they are not adults and cannot be treated as such. Compassion can make the difference inside classroom and I hope I am able to do more than just care for my students.

*Student Contemplation on a Praxis of Compassion #5*

My question is could teachers have too much compassion for their students? The student might take advantage of the teacher being so nice, and the teacher may not even realize it. I feel that if I was that teacher I would have given John a week before I made him go to his desk. I thought that a month was pushing it and the teacher was being too nice.

*Student Contemplation on a Praxis of Compassion #6*

First I would like to say that I hope I always remember the child under the desk because I believe that in my teaching career I will face many students that need to emerge from under the desk on their own terms. I hope that when the situations are presented to me in any form that I remember the story in that it is okay to allow the child to grow at his or her own pace. I hope I learn to work from compassion before protocol.

My understanding of the word compassion is much deeper now after reading this article. The visual of the physical joining to another person changed my idea of how extraordinary an act of compassion really is. To truly suffer inside for the pain of another and to forgo your power in hopes of easing a small piece of another person's pain, truly represent a union of great connection. After reading this I feel that compassion is when a person opens him or herself up in order to feel the pain of another so that a person doesn't have to suffer and face the pain alone.

*Student Contemplation on a Praxis of Compassion #7*

In the majority of my education courses, professors have stressed the importance of implementing various strategies and techniques in particular situations that occur in the classroom. While I agree that these methods and procedures are significant, I do not believe that they are the only components of an accurate behavior management plan. In fact, compassion is a vital element in the construction of a positive and successful behavior management plan. If implemented properly, a behavior management plan should be a way to analyze a situation and place yourself in your student's shoes and make adjustments that will better the student's overall state of mind.

*Student Contemplation on a Praxis of Compassion #8*

As I read the article I was deeply moved by the story of John and drawn to his teacher. I wondered if I would have been as compassionate. I wondered if I would have allowed him to hide under my desk. I wondered if I would have even thought to give him a flashlight to do his work, or if I would have been so concerned about the roles of school that I would have overlooked the role of compassion. I wonder.

So much of what I have learned in the years of caring for foster children involved behavioral management strategies, sticker charts, rewards and other incentives that were designed for the benefit of the child. For many children, the strategies work, but for many others they do not. Likewise the same types of behavior strategies have been lauded in several of the methods classes that I have taken here. While I understand the need for classroom management, isn't the management more for the teachers? If compassion is a witness of unconditional love, then teaching flows from the heart of the teacher to the students. The need for structure, while important in keeping pace with a particular curriculum, is an expression of the need in a child's heart for love and safety. Structure is not always about the rules. The claim made by William Ayres that teachers need to see each child in as full and complete a way as possible means to me that teachers need to engage the hearts of their students in order to know how they think. Learning isn't always reflected in what is taught formally. John learned much more about his value to the teacher and the value of compassion hiding under a desk than perhaps he would have ever learned otherwise. So did the other students. I want to be a teacher like John's. I want to inspire hope in the hearts of my students.

*Student Contemplation on a Praxis of Compassion #9*

This particular article struck a personal cord with me in terms of how I feel about children entering school and the teachers to which we entrust them. My daughter has a friend who has a mild case of Asperger's Syndrome. I was speaking to her mother one day about the issues concerning my son entering kindergarten and she shared a similar story with me. When her daughter initially went to kindergarten she became hysterical and hid under tables just like the child in the article. After about a week, the child was pulled out of school and held back one full year because the adults involved could not handle the situation. In this case it was not only the teacher but also the parent who was unable to express the compassion needed to help the child overcome the anxiety and frustration of entering school.

I feel that this article talks first and foremost about being a human being. In this case, the mother was not able to help the child so how could someone expect the teacher to have the ability to do so? The bottom line is that the teacher should have had the ability to work with the child and did not. As a parent I want to be able to send my children to an institution that I know will provide care and support for whatever situation arises. Teachers choose this profession knowing full well that they will be interacting with children for the majority of their day. Adults in general know that children can be difficult and will need extra attention or comfort at times. How can someone become a teacher without compassion? If you don't plan on putting forth your whole heart and soul into your work then you shouldn't be in a classroom.

Teachers have a responsibility to help the children that they encounter in the classroom and many children need more than just education while they are in school. The actions of the teacher in the article were not grand in the scheme of things to an adult, but it made a tremendous difference to that child. Too often adults react, most of the time badly and prematurely, to situations that they should first step back from and evaluate. It is far too easy to act without thinking, especially when it comes to children, because you do not want to lose control of the group; however it is because children are so unpredictable that you need to have the ability to use that second to ask if what you are about to do is the right thing for the situation. I feel that compassion is a trait that we all possess but something that we need to learn how to use effectively.

*Student Contemplation on a Praxis of Compassion #10*

I really loved reading this article because even though this is an education class, this piece of writing touched on a topic that is not often talked about in the education profession. I found the article *A Praxis of Compassion: A Contemplation*, to teach an extremely important lesson on the importance of being able to teach compassion to our future students. As you made the point very clear in your article, compassion is not as easily taught as unit plans or classroom management skills that are grounded in the behaviorism of educational practice. This tends to make something such as compassion so difficult to teach, because it is not a concrete concept that the children can simply memorize and then apply to a quiz or test. Compassion is something you learn through example, just as in the way this extraordinary teacher showed John in the article. John clearly exhibited terror and fear at the prospect of being in school, but nonetheless, the teacher would welcome him warmly and attempt to make John feel safe. I was so touched by the part in the article that talked about how the teacher would give John a blanket, pillow, and a flashlight to help him do his work while he stayed hidden under the teacher's desk. Rather than disciplining John, or using rewards and consequences to display a change in his behavior, she simply showed compassion. She allowed her caring feelings to show through her teaching strategies, and as an end result, John began to feel more comfortable and safe in the classroom. I have been taught to be compassionate toward others my entire life, and can only hope that I will one day be able to demonstrate my compassion for my student's in the self-less way that this teacher made it look so easy.

*Student Contemplation on a Praxis of Compassion #11*

With *A Praxis of Compassion* article I learned that I have a voice and it is okay to be critical, and not simply take in everything you learn. In this article there was a boy that was uncomfortable in the openness of the classroom and he sat under the teacher's desk; instead of the teacher scolding him she gave him a flashlight, a pillow and a blanket. The student slowly began to feel comfortable in the classroom and he inched his way from under the desk day by day. This was a wonderful story and it had a very positive ending. Yes, I wanted to be like that teacher, but in the back of my mind I was thinking that this type of reaction does not always work. That lead me to wondering, What if it didn't work? What if the other students started feeling as if I let him do what he wanted, so they would do what they wanted also? My main question was: Where does compassion end and being taken advantage of begin? Taking a chance on going against what I thought everyone else would say I thought I would be penalized for having my own opinion, but when I received my paper back my grade was just fine. This article reflection allowed me to understand that I am a critical thinker and it is okay to react critically.

*Student Contemplation on a Praxis of Compassion #12*

After reading *A Praxis of Compassion: A Contemplation,* I feel more confident to handle a situation with compassion and understanding. I give a lot of credit to John's teacher because I do not know if I would have reacted to that situation in the same way at first. Our goal as teachers is to reach out to the students, but how do we know how far to go? I understand and believe in the idea of letting the child work through the situation/problem…on his or her own, but would a school allow you to do this with a student? I would like to think so, but I feel with the pressures of state standards, they would not approve of a situation like John's. So when do you go against the protocol and follow your instincts? Following one's intuition can be very intimidating because it can go against the norm. However, standing up for your beliefs and being your students' advocate is your responsibility as a teacher.

Teaching is not just another everyday job. A teacher must be dedicated to his/her work and caring towards the students. Most of all, they must have compassion and understanding towards their students, providing a supportive environment where the student can feel safe to share what they are feeling. You must value and accept their opinions and feelings, and do not try to change them. Without compassion, a teacher will not be able to build a strong relationship with his/her students, resulting in uneasiness within the classroom. If the students do not feel like they can trust you, you will not be able to connect with them on an individual level.

Sometimes I worry about not being compassionate enough with my students and knowing what to do in situations, such as the one with John. The article says that "compassion is the capacity to enter into the experience of another person's life so fully that it enables me to respond in genuine communion and solidarity to the pain, difficulty, alienation, fragility, weakness, or suffering of another." Ultimately, it is taking the time to fully understand the situation and discover a way to work through it, not just finding a quick fix in the moment. There are no classes or workshops that you can take, teaching you how to act compassionately. One just has to embrace the opportunity and do what feels right in that moment. With experience and years of teaching, I think this will become a natural everyday way of teaching and living your life.

*Student Contemplation on a Praxis of Compassion #13*

After reading this article, I spent a great deal of time thinking about myself and what I would have done had I been in the same situation as John's teacher. I was amazed by the fact that she allowed this student to remain under her desk, every day, for the better part of a month because he was too afraid to come out and be a part of the classroom. I would like to think that I would have the ability to be reflective enough on the situation to allow the same type of thing to happen, but the truth of the matter is that I simply do not know.

When I think of the situation, I think not only of John under the desk, but also the rest of the class. What questions would the other students ask? What would administrators in the building think if they walked in to observe me teaching? Would I receive calls from other students' parents regarding the situation? I also think of myself. Would my need for control over the classroom environment overshadow my want to show compassion for my student? Would I be able to take a step back on that first day among all of the other stressors that I would be facing and deal with these things in an appropriate and compassionate manner? My hope is that I would.

I feel that the compassion that the teacher showed John is something that we do not often see in today's world. We live in a fast world that is overpowered by technology and our relational skills are often lagging. However, I also feel that in order to develop successful relationships with the other people in our lives, we need to have compassion for other beings and things.

I felt that consideration of what it would be like to include the ability to show compassion as a requirement for teacher certification was very interesting. So often we think of our time in school as simply getting through the theory of teaching and the content of the subjects. Teaching is so much more than that. In fact, sometimes I feel that teaching our students to be good citizens and sensitive human beings is more important than the actual subject matter. This is especially true for students who come from homes that do not provide these skills.

If we are able to show caring and compassion for our students, we will in turn help them to do the same for their peers and families. These skills are so important for each and every one of us to have, especially in today's world. John's teacher is someone that I hope to be like when I have my own classroom, and I plan to keep this article close for reference. I feel it will be helpful, especially in times when I feel challenged and frustrated.

*Chapter 5*

# Contemplation on Revelation—
# Curriculum in Process

## A Moment: Hidden from View

It was my first morning of work as a migrant health team member. We had travelled close to 1,000 miles to work for the summer in this far western region of South Carolina. Five of us climbed into the van and headed out of town on the two-lane highway. Paul immediately put a Willie Nelson tape into the console and pumped up the volume. We begged him to change the music. Our pleas for pop/rock music, which went unheeded, were soon forgotten as rows and rows of peach trees stretched out before us in all four directions for as far as we could see. Trucks and ladders were scattered throughout the fields. I was drawn to the almost undetectable movements of slender figures covered from the waist up by the peach tree branches. Paul pulled onto the shoulder of the road. From here we got a much closer look.

As we sat there, Paul talked about the history of the peach growers in the area and how it was that the migrants, most of whom were from central Florida or the Caribbean, came to the area each year. Occasionally, I caught a glimpse of a person climbing down from a ladder with a cotton sack slung over one shoulder. The weight of the bag pulled on their bodies as they quickly moved toward a large open backed truck. In one swift movement, the sack came rolling down from its resting place on the shoulder. Within seconds hundreds of peaches rolled out onto the pile of fruit. With a rapid turn of the heels, and an empty sack hanging at his or her side, one migrant worker after another repeated this ritual and then made his or her way back to the trees brimming with peaches.

We drove a little further and turned off a major highway onto a jagged country road. Hidden from view, but not far from the main highway sat one of the many migrant camps that I would encounter during the course of this summer. There is no universal description for a migrant camp. In trying to describe one I would have to describe them all; they were all different in some ways. If any commonalties can be ascribed to these migrant camps, it would be the overcrowded quarters, the lack of running water and indoor plumbing, and the unjust prices the people were charged to eat and to live in what, by most accounts, would easily be considered sub-standard and sub-human housing conditions.

Over the summer as I did blood screenings, I listened to people tell the stories of their families and how it was that they came to be migrant farm workers. They were fascinating persons, each with a unique story. There was no way to reduce their lives to sweeping statements and broad generalizations. Every camp was different; each story was unique; yet the common threads for them of economic needs and the struggle to survive were met by an extremely oppressive migrant structure in which they lived. I began to understand that every peach that I purchased at the grocery store contributed to perpetuating this structure of modern-day slavery. Why didn't we ever study this in school? Surely, it is as important as math or chemistry. Why didn't we learn about the daily injustices that were endured by men, women and children who were migrant farm workers?

Perhaps there was no time when this question haunted me more than the night a man and woman came to the clinic with their six-week-old baby who was very ill. We immediately took them to the emergency room and in spite of initially pleading and then fighting, the medical staff would not admit the baby. While they claimed that the baby was not ill enough to be hospitalized, we believed that the real reason was because the baby was both black and the child of migrant workers. The doctor in the emergency room recommended that we give the baby a particular type of formula and assured us that the child would be fine. We drove around the rest of the night in search of a store that was open. Finally, by early morning, we rushed out to the camp with the case of formula in our trunk. The baby was already dead. This precious baby had died in the night just a few short hours after being refused treatment in the hospital emergency room.

I was outraged. Every attempt to expose what had happened was suppressed by the local powers. Lies and denial proliferated as we confronted the small town authorities. Even those in Washington, DC, did not respond to our requests for an investigation.

I took a photograph of the small child in the coffin, the only request that the parents made, and gave it to them. There were only a few of us present to bury the baby in a small wooden box in a field behind a country church. No clergy would come. I said the prayers and blessed the body of this baby. As I threw the last bit of dirt over the coffin, I knew a rage inside of me like I had never before experienced.

There are nights when I am still awakened by the image of that tiny baby lying so still in the coffin.

## Author Contemplation on Revelation—Curriculum in Process

Many times over the course of the past 30 years baby William's face has appeared in my memory. A rupture occurred in my life at that moment. I had encountered structural injustice deeply embedded in cultural practices which were rooted in racism, sexism, and classism. So much of the way in which I would view the world from this point on would be through this experience.

I believe that William has forgiven me for not doing more to save his life; however, forgiveness is only one aspect of reconciliation. William's spirit continues to bring forth new revelations that demand that his memory be kept alive and remind me that the suffering and creative endurance of persons who have been subordinated and oppressed will not be quelled. His life still has a purpose and his spirit a message to offer. I have come to see how far William's spirit stretches me. His life-engaging spirit creates a motion in my soul that reminds me of my responsibility to respond to unmet human needs in whatever ways they are revealed. William's spirit speaks of the etymology of the word revelation, from the Latin, *revelatio*, meaning "to remove the veil" (Downey, 1993, p. 827). His death removed the veil many years ago and forced me to see the world in a way that I never had before witnessed. The revelation that William's life and death brought, lives in my life as a "source of enlightenment" and discloses "something previously unknown or not realized" (Simpson & Weiner, 1989).

Far-reaching implications were revealed to me as a result of knowing that a child died because of the colour of his skin, his economic class, and his parent's social status. I knew that the child of a white grower brought in with the same symptoms would have been admitted to the hospital and would have been alive the next day. It was not until I enrolled in a graduate level course in history a few years later that I ever studied forms of institutional and structural injustice within a broader historical framework. Janet James was the only woman professor that I had as an instructor in all of my undergraduate and graduate history courses. She was the one who transformed the two-semester American Social and Cultural History course into a curriculum that "removed the veil" by placing women, persons from various indigenous nations and groups, persons of color, ethnic groups, migrant workers, sharecroppers and others, who are normally omitted from history, at the center of the discourse. I remember Janet saying that it was very difficult to even find textbooks that included this perspective.

In looking at history through the lens of gender, race, and class, I was personally transformed. Our readings and discussions broke through the traditional categories of seeing how history had been constructed and organized. It was out of this experience that I would eventually structure the classes that I taught to young persons at the high school level. I realize now that in Janet James' classes we were engaged in what Jennifer Gore (1993) describes as the discourse of feminist pedagogy. It involved both the content and process of "(1) presenting 'new' texts, previously marginalized or overlooked within disciplinary knowledge; (2) engaging in 'new readings' of old texts...(3) drawing on the personal experiences of teacher and students as the basis of knowledge production" (p. 79). As a teacher, I have grappled with ways to invite the persons with whom I am learning into the discourse of feminist pedagogy and critical pedagogy. It has been my hope that in the process there would be both a personal transformation and a growing commitment toward creating a more just world.

One of the things that I learned over the course of these years from persons with whom I lived and worked, as well as from literature I have read, was that kindness and sensitivity were not enough to confront injustices. In an article entitled *The Demonization of Multiculturalism*, Richard Rorty (1995) argues that where attempts have been made in colleges and universities to include courses and programs in Hispanic studies, African-American studies and others like this, there is evidence that in turn there is greater respect and safety for blacks, browns, women, and gay and lesbian persons on these campuses. Rorty claims that

> A debilitating mistake was made, however, when academics began to campaign for compulsory undergraduate courses that would "sensitize students to cultural differences." Exercises in sensitivity often "boomeranged" as students became defensive and felt blamed for the problems of society. In contrast to such facile exercises in "sensitivity", genuine discussion about the divisions in American society would concentrate on disparities of power rather than differences in culture. (p. 74)

History and literature would be taught in such a way as to include the contributions of all. Additionally, the root causes of disparities of power would be addressed.

One of the tremendous challenges of teaching about persons who are oppressed is to not romanticize their lives or portray them as victims. The challenge for me as an educator is to develop the pedagogical frameworks that invite persons to understand the lives, culture and strength of persons in the margins while at the same time critically analysing the dominant center that produces those margins (hooks, 1984). In my initial attempts at doing this, I failed miserably. At first I was very didactic in my approach. Consequently, I was met with incredible reaction and resistance from many of the persons in class. I judged them to be morally unenlightened and intellectually shallow because they did not share either my understanding of the situation of persons working as migrant farm workers or my rage at their oppression. The harder I pushed for their understanding the more they resisted. Finally, I asked them about it.

A number of them told me that I was trying to shove things down their throats. I was very disturbed by the suggestion that I had created an oppressive environment through the way I was teaching about the injustices that existed in our society, where learners felt no freedom to interact or disagree. I had seen myself as very open. What I failed to acknowledge was the power I held in that classroom. I not only possessed the power to determine the curriculum, classroom structures, and grades, but also the power to control the ways ideas were shaped and shared.

For example, during a discussion I would immediately rebut what students said with an historical fact, statistic, or current reference instead of listening beyond what would be their words. I had a master's degree in history that I drew from for information and, whenever the students failed to see my point, I could easily reach into the knowledge bag that I carried for an impressive or intimidating piece of information. I began to realize how much I controlled what went on. At first, I justified my strong position believing that someone had to make the plight of persons who were systematically oppressed known; someone had to speak on their behalf. At what cost though? I began to understand that what for me was an attempt to expose and challenge perceived societal injustices was for many of the students an attack on many of the beliefs about

United States society that they were taught and held as important. I was asking them not only to question but also to reconstruct a knowledge base in which they had grown up and been schooled. I tried to deposit this information into their heads, and what I failed to realize was that this information challenged their very identity as white and primarily middle-class Americans. What I also failed to realize was that many of their ideas and insights stopped me and challenged me in a similar manner.

As I moved away from trying to convince students of a particular position and moved toward wanting to understand them, I slowly shed my arrogant and self-righteous attitude and gradually became more interactive and respectful of their views. Often the strength of ideological convictions, even when they are commendable, can still lead to a type of tyranny. I failed to recognize the dynamics of power in the classroom in the creation of new knowledge and was blind to the relationship between power and knowledge. I acted as though I was holding an open and free discussion, but it really wasn't. Even though I wasn't formally lecturing, I had my own little speech neatly packed away that I would regularly draw on in an attempt to bring them to my knowledge and my conclusion.

It is no wonder they experienced such oppression. I had known this same experience in my life, but failed to recognize that I was guilty of the same manipulation. As teachers it is hard not to succumb to this temptation. In trying to get students to embrace a justice perspective, I had relied on unjust structures. The stories of lives, struggles, and hopes need to be told and valued in the same way as calculus. The needs of persons who are denied access to economic and educational opportunities must be responded to in just and compassionate ways. Teaching is a compassionate, political and moral act. It is an act that can contribute to social change. However, the act of teaching must remain as just as the justice content that is being taught. Misgeld and Jardine (1989) offer the following challenge:

> If I am taken aback in a conversation with a child by the insightfulness and power of her questions, I cannot simply retreat into a self-possessed confidence in my ability to understand. Nor can I without hesitation simply banish the child's remark and turn away. Rather, my ability to understand is called into question. The "requisite skills" of adulthood are therefore not an impervious set of objective properties which I possess once and for all and in general, but interpretive possibilities that emerge in the concrete engagement with others. (p. 268)

Within classrooms, the nature of engagement with others is often shaped by implicit conversational norms. One long-standing norm places great value on classroom discussion where students are encouraged to share their experiences and points of view. As educator, Noreen Garman reminds us, however, discussion *per se* is no guarantee of authentic engagement with others or with our own preconceptions. This can be as true of teachers as of students. In *On Becoming a Dialogic Classroom: Walking the Path of Social Justice and Democracy*, Garman (2011) invites us to consider a distinction between classroom discussion and dialogic learning:

> During discussion, it's quite possible for participants to air their views on a particular subject didactically in order to get their positions heard, yet having no intention of engaging in a deliberative exchange by considering alternative views. Genuine deliberative dialogue requires that members of the group engage in and with each other's ideas, hearing, acknowledging, and considering facets of their own positions as well as the others'. Class members embody diverse backgrounds which include cultural and ideological experiences. Perhaps most important, university students are thought to bring with them their curiosity and capacity for learning. This means that a class member brings her/his

ability and energy to reason, to inquire, to interpret, to argue, to critique, to theorize...and above all, the desire to push the bounds of "everyday" intellectual activity. A member also brings the capacity to care about others, to find compassion in judgments and to see the humor, irony and inconsistencies in the human condition generally. These "capacities" are but a few that serve as the wellspring of energy for the time and space of the democratic classroom deliberations. (p. 4)

Yet, as I discovered, the temptation toward didactic moralism versus engaging dialogue is difficult to resist. Teaching requires imagination, energy, and vulnerability in order to move in the direction of generating discourse and creating knowledge as opposed to simply disseminating material and repeating information. Revelation as curriculum in process is incompatible with technical and behavioral models of school curriculum. Creating changes that move away from an information-based approach to school curriculum requires vision, curiosity, and conversation. I have come to see the tremendous power that the notion of revelation holds in relationship to curriculum that is shaped through an interactive human process.

One of the clearest concepts related to revelation as curriculum in process is within inquiry-based learning. At a conference entitled "Becoming a Learning Professional: Researching in the Workplace and the University," at The Flinders University of South Australia, Maria Piantanida's (1996) approaches to organizing curriculum are portrayed through a heuristic model. The four approaches represented in her heuristic model are: competency-based, information-based, inquiry-based, and problem-based. In regard to the inquiry-based approach Piantanida states:

The inquiry-based approach is organized around generative themes, fundamental issues that practitioners are likely to confront throughout their career—e.g., shifting social, political, and economic forces; mushrooming technology; decreasing "half-life" of knowledge; juggling personal and professional priorities. A curriculum organized around such themes emphasizes professional knowledge as exemplified by judgments, products, and performances. The assumption is that once students grasp the themes and begin to formulate questions about them, they have adopted a stance of reflective inquiry and are more likely to become self-directed, lifelong learners. (p. 4)

Piantanida expresses ideas related to the strengths and limitations of these different approaches. She suggests that some of the strengths in the inquiry-based approach are that it "develops proficiency in reflective practice, 'contextual knowing,' & inquiry-based learning…promotes tolerance for ambiguity & capacity for meaning-making." The limitations are that an inquiry-based approach "risks superficial & solipsistic thinking and makes standardized assessment difficult, perhaps impossible." (p. 4) An inquiry-based approach to curriculum embodies a structure that allows for revelation and opens up possibilities for enlightenment and disclosure of something not yet known or realized. Teachers and students construct knowledge together. Here on-going understanding comes through dialogue about what is revealed. While the teacher may possess a certain repertoire of information because of background and experience, he or she remains open and always enters into the learning process with the students as "co-inquirer" (Piantanida, 1996, p. 6) with a desire to "remove the veil."

When curriculum is seen as a process of revelation, a continuum of ideas in motion, then teacher/student and student/student relationships, as well as the purpose of conversation, discussion, and lecture take on a different significance than in an information-based approach. Revelation happens in the connections between persons, ideas, thoughts, feelings, stories. "Knowledge evolves in human relationships (Grumet, 1988, p. xix)." It is in the connections that things not previously understood can be revealed.

Drawing on the work of Jean Baker Miller in *Relational Cultural Theory* and Joyce K. Fletcher in *Relational Practice*[1], Harriet L. Schwartz and Elizabeth L. Holloway (2012) use the context of higher education to further extend the ideas of these theorists and offer fresh theoretical concepts. While the study focuses on meaningful academic relationships between adult master's students and their professors it is the last of their theoretical propositions, the connection paradox, that serves to illuminate the power of connections between persons engaged in learning relationships at every level of schooling. They argue that:

> Conventional wisdom would suggest that the closer we get to our students, the less able we are to set limits on the relationship, critically evaluate their work, and push them to work harder and reach higher. Along the same lines, one might assume that the closer we get to our students, the less able they are to see us in the context of our positions, the more casual they might treat the relationship, and even the lazier they may get regarding the work. I suggest that the inverse is true. Up and to a point (the line between a relationship that is ethical and one that is not), closer connection asks more of us, not less. Closer connection calls upon us as teachers to work harder at maintaining boundaries than we need to with the students with whom we are less connected. As we

---

[1] For information about *Relational Cultural Theory* and *Relational Practice* please refer to the works of Fletcher, J. K. (2001). *Disappearing acts: Gender, power, and relational practice at work*. Cambridge, MA: MIT Press. Fletcher, J. K., & Ragins, B. R. (2007). Stone Center relational cultural theory. In *The handbook of mentoring at work: Theory, research and practice* (pp. 373–399). Los Angeles, CA: Sage. Jordan, J. V. (2010). *Relational-cultural therapy* (1st edn.). Washington, DC: American Psychological Association. Miller, J. B. (1986). *Toward a new psychology of women* (2nd edn.). Boston, MA: Miller, J. B., & Stiver, I. P. (1997). *The healing connection: How women form relationships in therapy and in life*. Boston: Beacon Press.

work to challenge our students, closer connection can create a safe space so that amidst the challenges, students who feel safer may be more inclined to take bigger intellectual risks. Moreover, students who have experienced powerful connections with faculty have a taste of the richness of mutuality and collaboration, this is a motivating force which can evoke more and better work. Finally, students who experience and value these close connections with faculty, see the importance and uniqueness of these relationships and consciously express their respect for the positionality and boundaries that maintain the strength and definition of the relationship. Connection does not ask less of us as teachers and students, it asks far more of us all. (pp. 132-33)

Revelation as curriculum in process cannot be forced. It requires an understanding and respect for the person. Revelation as curriculum in process happens in the connections between persons.

## Student Contemplations on Revelation—Curriculum in Process

*Student Contemplation on Revelation—Curriculum in Process #1*

We all have backgrounds, views, and beliefs that shape and structure not only our learning experiences but the attitudes we carry throughout life. Many times when faced with an opposing view or a new learning experience, we shut down or become defensive of these views because they are not our own. The revelation process could be powerful and so insightful if only we let our guard down and allow ourselves the opportunity to become engulfed in the learning process—the true learning process of communication, understanding, and expanding knowledge and views. Within the school system, we are too focused on test scores and receiving federal aid than we are about engaging students in a type of learning that I personally have never seen in a textbook.

The inquiry approach to learning allows for communication between students and between student and teacher that is neither forced nor power-shifting. The 'power' of the classroom is not the teacher, but the experience. The communication is enlightening, not force-fed from the teacher upon the students. Everybody has equal access to input and allowing their views to be heard. A classroom should be a place where students feel safe to make mistakes or reveal their own understanding and views. It should be a place where students and teachers can feed off of each other and learn from each other. The course should be almost unpredictable in where it can go and what topics it can reach. The learning *process* is just that: a process. This process is a continuum of ideas that are on-going. Too many times teachers are focused on finishing a lesson to move on to the next topic. Teaching should not be about crossing off a list of activities mastered, but about connecting to students in a way where enlightenment and learning occur through revelation.

*Student Contemplation on Revelation—Curriculum in Process #2*

In today's schooling system, curriculum is monitored and decided upon depending on each district. There are many programs and content areas being decreased or eliminated altogether which in my opinion is hurting students. There are also different views and areas of the curriculum that are not being highlighted or incorporated. After reading *Revelation—Curriculum in Process*, I was impressed by many statements in the article.

Reading the personal experience Dr Llewellyn had while working with migrant workers and how it affected her made me realize how much we overlook certain issues either because of our beliefs or simply due to our ignorance and inability to look further into history and current events. Often, in schools we are taught history that has been meticulously planned or outlined in history books. We learn about the major wars, presidents, and other men and key events that help shape our society. It is rare to go beyond the events and learn about how people from different backgrounds affected the world. When we do learn about figures in history, we are taught what the history books depict as the truth. This was illustrated during a classroom activity where we read an excerpt from a fourth grade history book about Rosa Parks. In it Parks was portrayed as a poor, older woman who had a rough day. After reading the story we deconstructed the text using historical information about Rosa Parks that provided evidence that she was a strong, independent woman who was actively involved in the civil rights movement.

As teachers it is our job to bring to light those forgotten in our history. We are to connect curriculum to real world events for better understanding that can be applied in life. In doing this, I believe students will become more engaged in their learning and understand curriculum better. The article highlighted an inquiry-based instruction approach that focuses on generative themes that learners encounter throughout their lives whether in their education, occupation, or daily life. This approach allows for open discussions and reflections that ultimately have teachers and students construct knowledge together. The idea is that once the students understand the themes and generate the questions and reflections about them, they are more likely to become independent, open, lifelong learners.

I really appreciated that Dr Llewellyn admitted to having failed when trying to use a new approach in her class. It is one of my biggest fears to be an ineffective educator. However, I have come to understand that it is okay to make mistakes as long as you make it a learning process and have goals to become better. I admire that she got the opinions of her student and was able to openly take the criticism and advice and use it toward a better outcome. It is possible to go beyond the provided textbook and create a well-rounded classroom experience that impacts students and helps them become lifelong learners.

*Student Contemplation on Revelation—Curriculum in Process #3*

As I read the article, I became increasingly aware of the reason that I wanted to become a teacher. One of these reasons is to have the ability to bring about change in people's thinking, to influence them to see the best possible scenario for themselves and for the future of society in general. The many references and descriptions of injustices caused me to think of ways to bring about change. How can an individual influence a large number of people at the same time? Teaching is one of the ways that comes to mind.

    The author brings me back to earth when she remarks on the inability to control or change a group's way of thinking just by willing it. The article goes on to point out that what usually happens when one attempts this is opposition. You then defeat the whole purpose of teaching in the first place. To allow a student to feel that her/his opinion is worthy of discussion and that this viewpoint, although it may differ from the teacher's viewpoint, is vital. The author cautions that you cannot force your values on a group just because you have the power, you must respect the person and the place in which that person dwells both physically and emotionally. To be able to create an atmosphere in my own classroom that would allow open discussion, where each individual is valued, is my ultimate goal.

    The process of revelation as curriculum is constant, and valued, able to bring about the social change that must occur. Thinking about new ideas and awakening to the possibilities of other viewpoints is just as important a part of learning as the actual textbooks and measurable knowledge that students gain in the classroom. The awakening and surprise that awaits you when you open your heart and your mind is what I want my teaching career to embody.

*Student Contemplation on Revelation—Curriculum in Process #4*

As much as I would like to believe that kindness and sensitivity could act alone to correct injustices, this is just simply not true. Full understanding and acceptance of other cultures must be present to confront injustices in society. This is especially true in the classroom. When teaching about different cultures, a teacher must be very conscious of the way he or she presents this information. It is a tremendous challenge to not romanticize the lives of people who are oppressed or portray them as victims.

By reading this article, I discovered that it is difficult to ignore my own opinions and views when presenting information to the class. When introducing materials that deal with injustices, it must be responded to in just and compassionate ways.

*Student Contemplation on Revelation—Curriculum in Process #5*

I think that one of the most important things I was able to take from this piece is the challenge of effectively teaching in a way that encourages students to be open-minded without simply forcing our own opinions on our students. I really appreciated Dr Llewellyn's acknowledgement of her own struggles with this, as I see this as something I struggle with as well. I feel that it is extremely difficult not to let our own passions get in the way when teaching, especially with regards to social justice issues.

In order to be effective teachers who are able to successfully facilitate worthwhile conversation and learning, we must be willing to step off of the soapbox and listen to our students with an open ear and an open mind. By teaching in a way that is inquiry-based we are not simply talking at our students, we are growing with them and constructing knowledge together. As noted, this form of mutual respect and discussion is necessary for a successful classroom and I hope that I am to teach my own students with such care and respect.

*Student Contemplation on Revelation—Curriculum in Process #6*

The current state of education in the world is one that holds onto outrageous guidelines that leave the human being unattended and lacking in the opportunity to think critically. Llewellyn exposes the problems with the current curriculum enforced by our culture. She discovers troubles that exist in not only what is being taught but digs deeper to discover that the process in which curriculum is being taught contains a disruption to the human soul and eliminates the growth needed to change the world...The current curriculum does not encourage discussion of current practices in discrimination in terms of class, race, or social status. We are providing a disservice to students and the world by not exposing them or teaching them about the world they live in. How can we expect students to survive or advocate for themselves and others when we continually provide them with blinders?

Along with evaluating the content and process of the current curriculum, Llewellyn also discusses the challenges in how to teach in service of the student. Teaching must exhibit compassion and care. It must be difficult to convey the truth of the world with kindness and compassion, but as teachers, we have the responsibility to encourage young people to think abstractly and develop empathy for those who appear distant and disconnected. However we cannot remove the student's schemata. The experiences that follow individuals are unique and are to be valued. It is not our job as teachers to remove what they believe and the values they have come to shape their lives. Llewellyn claims, "creating changes that move away from an information base approach to school curriculum requires vision, curiosity, and conversation" (p. 4). When we engage with each other and value others' opinions as whole and true, we can progress towards changing the world collaboratively.

In addition, Llewellyn shines light on the pivotal need for revelation as curriculum. When students are provided within an inquiry-based approach to curriculum, they are empowered and the classroom can be transformed into the lifeline needed to create a meaningful and influential life. The classroom must be a community with multiple team members that are versatile, flexible, and valued for their knowledge and curiosity. When teachers and students work together, a respect for differences is invited to reveal the vitality and power in relationships. We are all connected to each other, no matter the extent of our differences. We are all human creatures who require the same basic human needs. When we are able to value and respect each other, we create a curriculum that will change the world. We are able to reveal the power of the human spirit when we see each other and understand that at the end of the day, we not only survive, but also grow and continually transform into person of strength, with the energy found in human connections.

*Student Contemplation on Revelation—Curriculum in Process #7*

This article highlighted the lack of gender, race and class issues included in school curricula. I appreciated the personal narrative at the beginning of the article in its direct connection to what is lacking in our educational system. The story about William and his family sparked controversial conversations about sexism, racism, and classism. I believe, after reading this article, that these upsetting, but true realities in our society should be included in the curriculum. I know that these issues are typically discussed in higher-level education courses, and although it may be difficult to discuss in classrooms with younger students, I am positive that the outcome of the students' global outlook will be beneficial, authentic and real. That should be the ultimate goal of the curriculum-authenticity, realism, and genuineness.

Another important factor in this article was the power that an educator has in any classroom and the control that he or she has over the curriculum and discussion. While at first Dr Llewellyn struggled with students understanding and agreeing with her opinions on social justice, she soon realized that a more interactive and respectful classroom would ultimately be more successful. I feel that as a new teacher I may struggle with the same difficulties that Dr Llewellyn faced in this particular situation, but if I keep in mind that everyone has her/his own story that is different and unique, I will be able to become more sympathetic and eventually have my students become more empathetic. I strongly believe that social injustices should be addressed and learned about in classrooms, but these issues cannot be addressed without mutual respect, consideration, and compassion for all.

At the end of the article, Dr Llewellyn discussed what I think is the most significant part of the article that is inquiry-based learning. The students become the inquirers and the teacher supports their interests and builds upon it. This is the key to revelation as curriculum. With this approach, learning is constant and every person in the classroom is valued and significant.

*Chapter 6*

# Contemplation on Being and Learning Together

**A Moment: Kindergarten**

"I want all eyes on me," the teacher yelled. "Now what's this colour?" My hand shot up immediately. I knew it was yellow.

"Jimmy," she asked looking right over my waving hand to the little boy who sat three seats behind me. "Yellow," said Jimmy.

"Say the color is yellow. Boys and girls, you must answer in a complete sentence," she said with her finger shaking and spanning out over the entire class in one clean sweep.

My mind wandered as I looked around the room and then through the front window onto First Street. "She always calls on the boys," I thought to myself.

The classroom itself was not colourful. A few decorations were hung around the room, but for the most part it was dull and stark. Each of us sat in a small wooden desk with a cold metal seat. The tiny holes in the metal seats, though not large enough to poke a pencil through, gave us a direct view of the floor making it very easy to find a lost pencil or a dropped crayon. The desks were on runners and lined up in row after row across the room.

A girl named Mary sat across from me. Silence was the classroom norm; so, Mary and I usually got to talk only during lunch time. I was vaguely aware that the teacher treated Mary differently. She usually either called on her as if she had done something wrong, or she ignored her totally. This day proved to be no different.

The bell rang for lunch. We ate quickly and then went outside to play. The afternoon bell rang, and we all marched in from the playground and lined up against the blackboard. The rule was that you had to go to the rest room after lunch whether you needed to or not. Experience had taught me that I better go now because it was hard to get permission for this later. We all made our way quickly and quietly to and from the boys' and girls' rooms.

The afternoon continued with lessons on letters and numbers. At one point Mary put her hand up before the teacher asked the next question. As usual, the teacher ignored her. Mary was dressed in a pretty plaid jumper with a white blouse that had a laced collar that looked slightly starched. Her hair was pulled back into two braids. Each had a tiny plaid bow that hung at the end of the braid and served to cover the rubber bands that kept the braids tight and together. She wore little white anklets and black shoes with bows. I hated being dressed up, but Mary actually made it look fun. Mary kept her hand raised while the teacher continued to ask questions and call on everyone but her. Mary's hand remained up in the air for what seemed like the longest time, yet the teacher continued to ignore her.

At one point I glanced over and saw big tears streaming down Mary's face. When I looked down at the puddle on the floor, I realized why Mary was crying. The moment the teacher recognized what had happened, she began to scream at Mary.

"It's not her fault. Mary had her hand up and you didn't call on her," I said without even thinking.

"Be quiet young lady or you will be in as much trouble as Mary," the teacher shouted at me.

"Mary had her hand up and you wouldn't call on her," I said in response. I was promptly corrected for "talking back."

The teacher walked to Mary's desk and whispered something to her that I didn't hear. Mary left the room with the teacher right on her heels. The teacher quickly returned with Mary who carried a bucket in one hand and a rag in the other. While Mary was down on her hands and knees scrubbing under her desk, the rest of the class continued to answer the teacher's questions about the alphabet as if nothing had happened.

I wanted to help Mary, but I remained frozen in my seat. I couldn't move; I couldn't even raise my hand. I'm not sure I can name what I was feeling at that moment. It might have been fear for me, embarrassment for Mary, disgust for the teacher or all three feelings creating an odd mixture of emotions that left me confused and sickened. I didn't feel safe until I was on the bus heading for home.

As soon as I walked in the door I blurted out to my mother everything that happened.

"You did the right thing and I'm proud of you for speaking up for Mary," she assured me.

I continued in school for a few more miserable weeks, but ended up dropping out of kindergarten before Thanksgiving.

I never saw Mary again. Yet the image of her brown face has never left me.

## Author Contemplation on the Classroom as Sacred Space

It was in kindergarten that I encountered racism for the first time, although I did not name it that at the time. Interestingly, Mary is the only classmate that I remember from my kindergarten class. What kind of a classroom space did Mary have to endure? What kind of classroom space did Mary deserve? What kind of a classroom does a child, an adolescent, an adult deserve? What kind of learning space places the learner at the center of the process and her/his educational journey?

Creating classroom spaces that are relational, safe, compassionate, nurturing and respectful is critical if we want to shape a learning environment that above all else values the learner at the center of the learning experience. Here the classroom is sacred space with the relationships between all learners rooted in faith. In tracing the etymology of the word "sacred" in the ancient world, Dudley Young (1991) contends that

> In the beginning supernatural power is experienced by primitive man as energy that interrupts or intensifies

the normal flow of events—an obvious example is the thunderstorm. By degrees, through the use of ritual and sympathetic magic, he seeks to harness this power so that it may animate and sustain the fabric of human orderliness that we call culture. …What are we to call this power?… The word favored by anthropologists since Durkheim's *The Elementary Forms of Religious Life* (1915) is "the sacred," denoting a range of experience set apart from and opposed to the everyday "profane" or "secular." (p. 309)

Young explores "five primitive locations or settings for the coming and going of divinity: the womb, the Jewish Ark of the Covenant, the hearth, the sacred wood at Nemi, and the dancing ground of Dionysus," all of which, except for the last one, he relates as "preliminary versions of the temple." Young connects the notion of these spaces "for the coming and going of divinity" (p. 209) as sacred.

From the five locations that Young described, I delved further into the womb and the hearth as precursors of the temple because these were intriguing to me in light of my own contemplations. Young relates that

*Temenos* in Greek means either an estate, an area of ground sacred to some god, or else the precincts of a temple. Long before we began thinking of temples, however, or even of making rules restricting the use of our dancing ground, we would have realized that Nature herself had provided our first sacred space in the woman's womb. (p. 210)

For a couple of years I was the guidance counsellor in the high school where I taught. A large storage closet had been turned into the Guidance Office. In the office there were wooden shelves that lined the walls, a small desk, a file cabinet, and a table with about six chairs around it. Some of the seniors began to fondly refer to this space as "the womb." A couple of them asked if they would be allowed to come into the Guidance Office during their study hall and do their work in there. I told them it was fine with me as long as they cleared it with the study hall teacher, and I could still get my work done. Every week they checked in with the study hall teacher and then proceeded to come to the Guidance Office for the 50 minute study period. They would read, do homework assignments, and agonize over calculus. We were generally very quiet, although occasionally one of us might interrupt the silence to share some humorous thought or funny story. One day as we sat there doing our work, I looked over at them and curiously asked, "Why do you like to study in here?" All of them looked up at me and uttered different responses. They said "It's nice in here; it's cool; it's quiet; it's comforting; it's the womb." While at the time I was struck by the student's remark "It's the womb," it was only much later that I came to recognize that when the students referred to the Guidance Office as "the womb," they were drawing on a mythic way of knowing. In a tacit way the students were expressing an understanding that certain space that embodies comfort is connected to a "reverence for the womb as sacred space" (Young, 1991, p. 217).

Space that allows for the powers within persons to have room to emerge is space that is rendered sacred. Learning places where each person is responsible for his/her own learning and, in turn, feels responsible for the learning of one another is space made sacred. I thought of the ways in which John's teacher rendered the space beneath her desk sacred through her way of being with John. She was being-with-compassion. The notion of space made sacred draws on the wisdom of the ancients where "Because myth relates the gesta of Supernatural Beings and the manifestation of their sacred powers, it becomes the exemplary model for all significant human activities" (Eliade, 1963, p. 6). The boundaries of the sacred space of the woman's womb are extended in new dimensions as space is rendered sacred through compassion and love. A place beneath a desk or a classroom where persons are valued for who they are more than what they achieve is space made sacred through significant human exchange.

Young's discussion of the hearth is very poignant in the way that it speaks of sacred space. Another prologue to the temple is the hearth, the fire around which we gather to eat together and offer hospitality to the stranger. The hearth is sacred not only because it is a space in which we remember the tribal or household gods, but more simply because it is where weapons may be confidently set aside while the bonds of kinship are ritually renewed in giving and taking. (p. 214) For a child or adolescent being welcomed into a place of comfort and safety helps to bring about bodily calm and inner peace. Here the classroom is a type of contemporary hearth. Around this hearth, hospitality, comfort, and safety are central. With all of the activity, motion, pressure and outside forces that young people experience, there is little natural time in their day when reaching bodily calm and inner peace, as opposed to sitting still in one's desk, are valued.

In the high school where I taught, the students had to move every 50 minutes from one subject to another, sometimes covering as many as seven different subjects a day. Even in a small high school such as this, students were often taught by many different teachers with vastly different expectations. During the course of any given day, teachers also can encounter as many as 150 different students all with various needs and learning styles. Given such demands, teachers also indicate that it is just as difficult for them as it is for students to achieve a bodily calm and inner peace during the course of a normal school day. In order to encourage young persons to lift up their spirit, I am required to consistently restore my own spirit and to make visible and celebrate my own essence. What is needed in education today are not higher standards evaluated primarily through more testing, increased information, stricter codes of discipline, expanded programs, and enhanced formulas for behavior management, but a growing sense of the classroom as the hearth, a sacred space where the stranger is welcomed, the learner's educational journey is central, life memories are shared, and transformation is possible through our way of being with one another. Space is rendered sacred in the ordinary ways that we relate to each other.

Theories of childhood and beliefs about children/youth can keep space from being sacred. Barrie Thorn's (1994) analysis of the way adults view children at times speaks to ways that block creating sacred space. Thorne says

> ...it is hard to think of one's self as a novice when studying those who are defined as learners of one's own culture. To learn *from* children, adults have to challenge the deep assumption that they already know what children are "like," both because, as former children, adults have been there, and because, as adults, they regard children as less complete versions of themselves. When adults seek to learn about and from children, the challenge is to take the closely familiar and to render it strange. (p. 12)

The denial of children/young people's experiences and thought creates power relations of domination and prevents space from being sacred.

The experiences of all members of a group are central to the creation of a sacred space. The sharing of power is critical in creating sacred space where a participatory process of listening and talking to one another is at the heart of the vision. Whenever persons enter into unfamiliar spaces and attempt to think and learn in new ways, there can be awkwardness, yet moving with integrity and being open to a connection with others can render these spaces sacred. Closed and controlled spaces prevent the sacred from taking shape. Making a space sacred is related to a view of power. In her book *Teaching to Transgress*, bell hooks (1994) claims:

> Fearful that I might abuse power, I falsely pretended that no power difference existed between students and myself. That

was a mistake. Yet it was only as I began to interrogate my fear of "power"—the way that fear was related to my own class background where I had so often seen those with class power coerce, abuse, and dominate those without—that I began to understand that power was not itself a negative. It depended what one did with it. It was up to me to create ways within my professional power constructively, precisely because I was teaching in institutional structures that affirm it is fine to use power to reinforce and maintain coercive hierarchies.

Fear of losing control in the classroom often leads individual professors to fall into a conventional teaching pattern wherein power is used destructively. It is this fear that leads to collective professorial investment in bourgeois decorum as a means of maintaining a fixed notion of order, of ensuring that the teacher will have absolute authority. (pp. 187-188)

This form of control prevents the creation of sacred space. The sacred has been defined too narrowly. Boundaries need to be stretched to include ordinary space that is rendered sacred by meaningful and powerful human exchanges. While challenging in the current climate of testing and standardization, it is imperative that we create learning communities where trust is a central value for all involved. (Meier, 2002) When Freire (1983) claims that "the teacher is no longer merely the one-who-teaches, but one who is himself taught in dialogue with the students, who in turn while being taught also teaches" (p. 288), he is reflecting a central dimension of being and learning together. The teacher/learner relationship is one of mutuality in which one cannot grow without the other.

## Author Contemplation on Wisdom and Hope

In the darkness and silence of early morning contemplations, I still come face to face with Mary and see the pain and humiliation in her eyes once again. Through being with Mary, working with persons in the Migrant Camps, taking the Book Mobile from door-to-door at the Kelly Street high-rise, and teaching young persons in school, the divine wisdom of lived experience and holding onto hope become vividly important.

The word wisdom, as utilized in theology and Scripture, comes from the Latin word *sapientia* which is derived from the word *sapere*, meaning to taste and to savour (Downey, 1993). The Oxford English Dictionary further describes wisdom in the following ways: "capacity of judging rightly in matters relating to life...knowledge; enlightenment, learning, erudition." Wisdom makes understanding possible when we dwell on a lived experience in such a way as to taste and savour the meanings that it reveals. Within the current educational rhetoric, it is rare to come across the notion of wisdom as being a valuable aspect of what happens in schools. Alfred North Whitehead (1929) noted that:

> In the schools of antiquity the philosopher aspired to impart wisdom, in modern colleges our humbler aim is to teach subjects. The drop from the divine wisdom, which was the goal of the ancients, to text-book knowledge of subjects, which is achieved by the moderns, marks an educational failure sustained through the ages...What I am anxious to impress on you is that though knowledge is one chief aim of intellectual education, there is another ingredient, vaguer but greater, and more dominating in its importance. The ancients called it 'wisdom.' (pp. 45-46)

Whitehead's point is illustrated in this conversation that I had with a young woman in a college class that I was teaching. She wasn't sure if she had done the assignment "right" and wanted to talk about it. The assignment was an autobiographical free-write that asked students to reflect on their own experiences of education and then write about them. Although this person had come to understandings through reflecting on her lived experience, she was afraid that she had done the assignment incorrectly. She had included her personal-life and home-life in her writing and had shared much of what was going on outside of school in the reflection. She shared with me that what was happening outside of school was so intense that in many ways it overshadowed what she remembered about school. While she had learned things from writing about her lived experience, she questioned whether this kind of material belonged in an educational assignment. One of the aspects of her story that reflected divine wisdom was her realization that the reading books they used were so removed from her experience of family that it reinforced the illusion that this was what real families were like. Each day she lived with the hope that her family would become like the family in her reader. This never happened.

Much of what actually takes place in young persons' lives is not valued or reflected in our schools. At the age of five, I had ventured away from the safety and security of my neighborhood and headed into town to attend kindergarten. I had no awareness that in the previous year on May 17, 1954, the Supreme Court had issued a unanimous ruling insuring that Linda Brown, a seven-year-old from Topeka, KS, had a legal right to attend an integrated school. While Brown vs. The Board of Education ensured blacks the right to make choices about their child's education, it didn't ensure that the environment in schools their children attended would be just. Over 50 years after Brown vs. the Board of Education, I am still encountering on a regular basis incidents of racism in schools through stories reflecting the attitudes held by teachers and students. They are a powerful testimony to the deeply rooted practices of racism displayed in our day-to-day living. I have come to believe that creating spaces for the divine wisdom of lived experience to be shared in classrooms is critical if we want a greater understanding among persons, particularly in dealing with differences and valuing one another.

While working with a group of high school students on a program that addressed issues of prejudice, I witnessed the power that sharing the divine wisdom of lived experience offered in many of our classroom exchanges. The young persons were asked to share personal experiences of prejudice related to issues of gender, class, race and disability. After extending an invitation to share, there would often be a period of silence. I imagined that the silence came because some of the students were trying to recall their own experience of prejudice while others whose experiences quickly rose to the surface were weighing whether it was worth the risk of sharing what had been rendered a private matter in such a public way.

On one such occasion, Lisa began the conversation by stating that many of her teachers in school had been prejudiced. She shared an experience that she had with her kindergarten teacher that had hurt, angered, and humiliated her. Her story was short, and in a few moments I was led into disturbing levels that evoked horror, embarrassment, deep sorrow, and anger.

"The teacher never allowed the African-American children to lie on the cots to take our naps. We had to sit in our wooden desks with our heads down. Did she think that our skin colour would rub off and stain the sheets brown?" Lisa asked.

She said these words with a deep hurt that was still evident in her voice and a hint of embarrassment at the humiliation that this action had caused day after day so many years ago. Later she told me that having a space within which to share this experience with others strengthened her courage.

In another class we were discussing what influenced white persons to be prejudiced. After various comments were shared, one young woman raised the question as to whether African-Americans could be prejudiced. Another discussion ensued in which various opinions were put forth for consideration. At one point in the discussion, Patricia shared that her aunt was extremely prejudiced against white people. Patricia mentioned that while she did not hold comparable attitudes, she understood why her aunt was so hostile. I was not prepared for what she would share next. Patricia mentioned that most of her family lived in the south. She then shared that the reason that her aunt hated whites so much was because she had watched her five sons being lynched. There was silence in the room. Tears running down my cheeks blurred the words I had written in the notebook. Unable to write another word, I put my pen down and looked around at the faces of the young people in that classroom.

Even though I resisted thinking about what Lisa and Patricia had shared, their words kept drawing me to various places within myself—places that hovered between the conscious and subconscious, places that moved between guilt and despair, places that lingered between suffering and reconciliation, places that cried for transformation, and shadowy places stilled unnamed. Initially, I felt an overwhelming sense of hopelessness. I could barely think about the details of the stories each had shared. I could only see the image of white sheets. It created a persistent presence in my mind until one day I wrote a poem about what had been shared in the classroom. At first the poem was only a few words, but then gradually it took a shape.

**White Sheets**

Two young women recall the past
    a classroom
        a field
            human pain
White sheets carve memories etched in souls
White sheets bring terror in the night

Fiery wood and torches burning bring the only light
Fire embraces cross
Whips bludgeon skin
Crackling leather on human flesh
She looks on in agony at one
                    two
                          three
                                four
                                      five

Those whom she called son
Limp and lifeless bodies now
Eyes from within her soul watch
As her own flesh hangs from a rope

Kindergarten children nap on cots and crisp white sheets
Not all though
The young girl asks
Does she think our skin rubs off
and makes the white sheets dirty?
Tears roll down her cheeks
No one noticed

Maxine Greene (1995a) contends that "Education, after all, has to do with engaging live human beings in activities of meaning-making, dialogue, and reflective understanding of a variety of texts, including the texts of their social realities" (p. 305). It is rare to encounter students' social realities as valued texts in our classrooms the way that commercially produced textbooks are honoured. When the divine wisdom of lived experience is valued and incorporated in our classrooms, it opens up the possibility for hope and encourages the kind of meaning-making of which Greene speaks. In their book *Teaching the Taboo*, Rick and William Ayers (2011) ask if we can imagine dramatically different schools by cutting through the barriers, boundaries, and taboos that characterize schooling today. They write:

> Our invitation is to live a teaching life of questioning, to imagine classrooms where every established and received bit of wisdom, common sense, orthodoxy, and dogma is open for examination, interrogation, and rethinking. The process of upending begins at the beginning: *why*? This simple word challenges every authoritarian impulse and every autocratic structure everywhere: *why*?

The provocation builds on that invitation: Can we construct our school and classroom practices on the base of fearless and relentless inquiry? For every confounding and repressive aspect of school as we find it, can we imagine something better? Can we see standing directly next to the situation as it is, the situation as it could be or should be? That is for us the point of first departure for teaching the taboo. (p. 2)

Living into the questions, remaining open to the *why* in every moment and walking a path of inquiry is a way of being and learning together in sacred spaces.

My intent in this book has been to articulate a spirituality of teaching where learning and the learner is at the heart of the endeavour. My hope is to offer ways of thinking about pedagogy that help to envision another educational world than the one that currently exists. Given all of the complexity in our contemporary world, can understanding a spirituality of teaching as it connects to placing learning and the learner at the center help shape education in ways that respond to those challenges? I recognize how easy it is for me to lose sight of the importance of creating space for acceptance, faith, knowledge and wisdom to reside together. In the current educational climate it is challenging to engage in a praxis of compassion when confronted with the reality of standardization. It is difficult to hold on to hope in the face of so much educational reform gone awry. New metaphors are needed to shape an understanding of schools as being places where growing as a human being is of the utmost value and learning is a human encounter rooted in relationships marked by faith, trust, compassion and love.

# References

Astell, A. W. (1996/Summer). Postmodern Christian spirituality: A co-incidentia oppositorum. *Christian Spirituality Bulletin, 4*(1), 2-5.

Ayers, R., & Ayers, W. (2011). *Teaching the taboo: Courage and imagination in the classroom.* New York: Teachers College Press.

Ayers, W. (1995). Becoming a teacher. In W. Ayers (Ed.), *To become a teacher: Making a difference in children's lives* (pp. 5-9). New York: Teachers College Columbia University.

Bevis, W. W. (1988). *Mind of winter: Wallace Stevens, meditation, and literature.* Pittsburgh, PA: University of Pittsburgh Press.

Blumenfeld-Jones, D. (1996). Conventional systems of classroom discipline (The patriarchy speaks). *Journal of Educational Thought, 30*(1), 5-21.

Brehony, K. A. (1996). *Awakening at midlife: A guide to reviving your spirit, recreating your life, and returning to your truest self.* New York: Riverhead Books.

Brown, J. (1992). Theory or practice: What exactly is feminist pedagogy? *Journal of General Education, 41*, 51-63.

Cannon, K. G. (1988). *Black womanist ethics* (Vol. 60). Atlanta, Georgia: Scholars Press.

Capra, F. (1996). *The web of life: A new scientific understanding of living systems.* New York: Anchor Books Doubleday.

Cleage, A. B. (1968). *The black Messiah.* New York: Sheed and Ward.

Cone, J. H. (1969). *Black theology and black power.* New York: Seabury Press.

Cooper, A. J. (1988). *A voice from the South* (originally published 1892 ed.). New York: Oxford University Press.

Cuban, L. (2004). Looking through the rearview mirror at school accountability. In K. A. Sirotnkin (Ed.), *Holding accountability accountable: What ought to matter in public education* (first ed., pp. 18-34). New York Teachers College Press.

Downey, M. (Ed.). (1993). *The new dictionary of Catholic spirituality*. Collegeville, MN: The Liturgical Press.

Duhon-Sells, R., Sells, H., & Mouton, A. (1997). Peace education: Enhancing caring skills and emotional intelligence in children. In R. Duhon-Sells (Ed.), *Exploring self science through peace education and conflict resolution* (Vol. 6, pp. 1-13). Lewiston, NY: The Edwin Mellen Press.

Eisner, E. (1985). Aesthetic modes of knowing. In E. Eisner (Ed.), *Learning and teaching the ways of knowing* (pp. 23-36). Chicago, IL: The University of Chicago Press.

Eliade, M. (1963). *Myth and reality* (W. Trask, Trans.). New York: Harper & Row.

Freire, P. (1970). *Pedagogy of the oppressed*. New York: Seabury Press.

Freire, P. (1983). The banking concept of education. In H. Giroux & D. Purpel (Eds.), *The hidden curriculum and moral education* (pp. 283-291). Berkeley, CA: McCutchan.

Garman, N. B. (1990). The closed and open contract: Two irreconcilable structures in the curriculum. *Journal of the World Council for Curriculum and Instruction, IV*(2), 176-182.

Garman, N. B. (1994, August 5, 1994). *Qualitative research: Meaning and menace for educational researchers.* Paper presented at the Qualitative Approaches in Educational Research, The Flinders University of South Australia.

Garman, N. B. (2011). On becoming a dialogic classroom: Walking the path of social justice and democracy. Unpublished Work.

Garrison, J. (2010). Compassionate, spiritual, and creative listening in teaching and learning. *Teachers College Record 112*(11), 2763-2776.

Goba, B. (1990). What is faith? A black South African perspective. In S. Brooks Thistlethwaithe & M. Potter Engel (Eds.), *Lift every voice: Constructing Christian theologies from the underside* (pp. 21-30). New York: HarperSanFrancisco.

Gore, J. (1993). *The struggle for pedagogies: Critical and feminist discourses as regimes of truth*. New York: Routledge.

Greene, M. (1995a). Educational visions: What are schools for and what should we be doing in the name of education? In J. L. Kincheloe & S. R. Steinberg (Eds.), *Thirteen questions: Reframing education's conversation*. New York: Peter Lang.

Greene, M. (1995b). *Releasing the imagination*. San Francisco: Jossey-Bass Publishers.

Griffin, D. R. (1988). Introduction: Postmodern spirituality and society. In D. R. Griffin (Ed.), *Spirituality and society: Postmodern visions* (pp. 1-31). Albany, New York: State University of New York Press.

Grumet, M. R. (1988). *Bitter milk: Women and teaching*. Amherst: The University of Massachusetts Press.

Hardman-Cromwell, Y. C. (1995). Living in the intersection of womanism and Afrocentrism: Black women writers. In C. J. Sanders (Ed.), *Living the intersection: Womanism and Afrocentrism in theology* (pp. 192). Minneapolis: Fortress Press.

Hayes, D. (1995). *Hagar's daughters, womanist ways of being human*. New York: Paulist Press.

hooks, b. (1984). *Feminist theory: From margin to center*. Boston: South End Press.

hooks, b. (1994). *Teaching to trangress: Education as the practice of freedom*. New York: Routledge.

Huebner, D. (1975a). Curricular language and classroom meanings. In W. Pinar (Ed.), *Curriculum theorizing: The Reconceptualists* (pp. 217-236). Berkeley, CA: McCutchan Publishing.

Huebner, D. (1975b). Curriculum as concern for man's temporality. In W. Pinar (Ed.), *Curriculum theorizing: The reconceptualists* (pp. 237-249). Berkeley, CA: McCutchan Publishing Corporation.

Huebner, D. (1975c). The tasks of the curricular theorist. In V. Hillis (Ed.), *The lure of the transcendent: Collected essays by Dwayne E. Huebner* (pp. 212-230). Mahwah, New Jersey: Lawrence Erlbaum Associates.

Huebner, D. (1983). Religious metaphors in the language of education. *Religious Education, 80*(3), 460-472.

Huebner, D. (1984). The Search for Religious Metaphors in the Language of Education. *Phenomenology + Pedagogy, 2*(2), 112-123.

Huebner, D. (1985). Spirituality and knowing. In E. Eisner (Ed.), *Learning and teaching the ways of knowing* (Vol. Eighty-fourth, pp. 159-173). Chicago: The University of Chicago Press.

Huebner, D. (1995). Education and Spirituality. *Journal of Curriculum Theorizing, 11*(2), 13-34.

Huebner, D. (1999a). *The lure of the transcendent: Collected essays by Dwayne E. Huebner.* Mahwah: Lawrence Erlbaum.

Huebner, D. (1999b). Teaching as a Vocation. In V. Hillis (Ed.), *The Lure of the Transcendent: Collected Essays by Dwayne E. Huebner* (pp. 379-387). Mahwah, New Jersey: Lawrence Erlbaum Associates.

Joseph, G. (1995). Black feminist pedagogy and schooling in capitalist white America. In B. Guy-Sheftall (Ed.), *Words of fire: An anthology of African-American feminist thought* (pp. 462-471). New York: The New Press.

Kovel, J. (1991). *History and spirit: An inquiry into the philosophy of liberation.* Boston: Beacon Press.

Kozol, J. (1995). *Amazing grace: The lives of children and the conscience of a nation.* New York: Crown Publishers, Inc.

Kreisberg, S. (1992). *Transforming power: Domination, empowerment, and education.* Albany, New York: State University of New York Press.

Lernoux, P. (1989). *People of God: The struggle for world Catholicism.* New York: Penguin Books.

Macdonald, J. B. (1995). *Theory as a prayerful act: The collected essays of James B. Macdonald* (Vol. 22). New York: Peter Lang.

Macdonald, J. B. (1995). A vision of a humane school. In B. J. Macdonald (Ed.), *Theory as a prayerful act: The collected essays of James B. Macdonald* (Vol. 22, pp. 49-67). New York: Peter Lang.

Maturana, H. R., & Varela, F. J. (1980). *Autopoiesis and cognition: The realization of the living* (Vol. 42). Dordrecht: Holland/Boston: USA: D. Reidel Publishing Company.

McWilliam, E. (1996). Introduction: Pedagogies, technologies, bodies. In E. McWilliam & P. G. Taylor (Eds.), *Pedagogy, technology, and the body* (Vol. 29, pp. 1-22). New York: Peter Lang.

Meier, D. (2002). *In schools we trust: Creating communities of learning in an era of testing and standardization.* Boston: Beacon Press.

Miller, J. P. (1994). *The contemplative practitioner: Meditation in education and the professions.* Westport, CN: Bergin & Garvey.

Misgeld, D., & Jardine, D. (1989). Hermeneutics as the undisciplined child: Hermeneutic and technical images in education. In M. J. Packer & R. B. Addison (Eds.), *Entering the circle: Hermeneutic investigation in psychology* (pp. 259-273).

Noddings, N. (1995). *Philosophy of education.* Boulder, CO: Westview Press, Inc. A Division of HarperCollins Publishers.

Omolade, B. (1993). A black feminist pedagogy. *Women's Studies Quarterly, XXI*(3&4).

Piantanida, M. (1996, May 10, 1996). *Reflections on curriculum and instruction in professions education: A heuristic model.* Paper presented at the Becoming a Learning Professional: Researching in the Workplace and the University, Flinders Institute for the Study of Teaching, The Flinders University of South Australia.

Radford Ruether, R. (1992). *GAIA and God: An ecofeminist theology of earth healing.* New York: HarperSanFrancisco--A Division of HarperCollins Publishers.

Radford Ruether, R. (1996). Introduction. In R. R. Ruether (Ed.), *Women healing earth: Third World women on ecology, feminism, and religion*. Maryknoll, NY: Orbis Books.

Ravitch, D. (2010). *The death and life of the great American school system: How testing and choice are undermining education*. New York: Basic.

Rich, A. (1979). When we dead awaken: Writing as re-vision. In A. Rich (Ed.), *On lies, secrets, and silence: Selected prose 1966-1978* (pp. 33-49). New York: W. W. Norton & Company.

Richardson, L. (1990). Narrative and sociology. In *Representation in ethnography* (pp. 198-221). Thousand Oaks, CA: SAGE.

Riggs, M. Y. (1994). *Awake, arise, & act: A womanist call for black liberation*. Cleveland, Ohio: The Pilgrim Press.

Rorty, R. (1995). The demonization of multiculturalism. *The Journal of Blacks in Higher Education, Spring*(7), 74-75.

Schoonmaker, F. (2009). Only those who see take off their shoes: Seeing the classroom as a spiritual space. *Teachers College Record 111*(12), 2713-2731.

Schüssler Fiorenza, E. (1996). *The power of naming: A Concilium reader in feminist liberation theology*. Maryknoll, NY: Orbis Books.

Schwartz, H. L., & Holloway, E. L. (2012). Partners in learning: A grounded theory study of relational practice between master's students and professors [Electronic Version]. *Mentoring & Tutoring: Partnership in Learning, 20*, 115-135. Retrieved 25 February 2012, from http://dx.doi.org/10.1080/13611267.2012.655 454.

Shrewsbury, C. (1993). What is feminist pedagogy? *Woman's Studies Quarterly, XXI*(3&4).

Simpson, J. A., & Weiner, E. S. C. (Eds.). (1989). *The Oxford English dictionary* (Second ed.). Oxford: Clarendon Press.

Smith, D. G. (1999). *Pedagon: Interdisciplinary essays in the human sciences, pedagogy, and culture* (Vol. 15). New York: Peter Lang.

Steiner, R. (1995). *The spirit of the Waldorf school: Lectures surrounding the founding of the first Waldorf school* (N. P. Whittaker, Trans. Originally published in Stuttgard in 1919 ed.). Hudson, NY: Anthroposophic Press.

Thorne, B. (1994). *Gender play: Girls and boys in school.* New Jersey: Rutgers University Press.

Townes, E. M. (1993). *Womanist justice, womanist hope* (Vol. 79). Atlanta Georgia: Scholars Press.

Townes, E. M. (1995). *In a blaze of glory: Womanist spirituality as a social witness.* Nashville: Abingdon Press.

Trible, P. (1978). *God and the rhetoric of sexuality.* Philadelphia: Fortress.

van Manen, M. (1991). *The tact of teaching: The meaning of pedagogical thoughtfulness.* New York: State University of New York Press.

Vaughan, F. E. (1979). *Awakening intuition.* New York: Anchor Books, Doubleday.

Weiler, K. (1991). Freire and a feminist pedagogy of difference. *Harvard Educational Review, 61*(4), 449-474.

Whitehead, A. N. (1929). *The aims of education and other essays.* New York: The Macmillan Company.

Williams, D. S. (1993). *Sisters in the wilderness: The challenge of womanist God-talk.* Maryknoll, NY: Orbis Books.

Woodson, C. G. (1933/1993). *The mis-education of the Negro.* Trenton, NJ: Africa World Press, Inc.

Wyschogrod, E. (1990). *Saints and postmodernism.* Chicago: University of Chicago Press.

Young, D. (1991). *Origins of the sacred: The ecstasies of love and war.* New York: St. Martin's Press.

## Learning Moments Press

Learning Moments Press is a small, independent publishing company dedicated to sharing the wisdom that comes from thoughtful reflection on experience. The Wisdom of Practice Series showcases the work of individuals who illuminate the complexities of practice as they strive to fulfill the purpose of their profession.

Cooligraphy artist Daniel Nie created the logo for Learning Moments Press by combining two symbol systems. Following the principles of ancient Asian symbolism, Daniel framed the logo with the initials of Learning Moments Press. Within this frame, he has replicated the Adinkra symbol for *Sankofa* as interpreted by graphic artists at the Documents and Designs Company. As explained by Wikipedia, Adinkra is a writing system of the Akan culture of west Africa. *Sankofa* symbolizes taking from the past what is good and bringing it into the present in order to make positive progress through the benevolent use of knowledge. Inherent in this philosophy is the belief that the past illuminates the present and that the search for knowledge is a life-long process.

www.ingramcontent.com/pod-product-compliance
Lightning Source LLC
Chambersburg PA
CBHW050542300426
44113CB00012B/2220